Victory Over Fear

Breaking Free
and Embracing Triumph

By
Rejoice Anusi

First printing, 2024.

Publishing Company
Wilson Paper Co.
1550 Wilson Boulevard
Suite 700
Arlington, VA 22209

www.wilsonpaperco.com

TABLE OF CONTENTS

CHAPTER ONE
MY FAITH
STORY:
THE ACCIDENT

"Traumas are strongholds that can limit you from moving forward. Sometimes we don't know how it indirectly affects other areas of our lives."

I can't count how many times God has shown up for me, even when I felt like I was reaching the point of death. From my very early years in life, the enemy always found a way to come in and take over; but God has always stood in for me! When I was seven (7), I had a terrible accident on the highway that almost took my life. I will never forget that sunny afternoon coming home from elementary school, Airforce Primary School, Port Harcourt, with other pupils. It was just a ten to fifteen-minute walk from where we lived to my school. Alot of kids in our neighborhood attended the same school so we all returned from school together.

On a normal day, there would be military men around to stop cars and ensure the kids crossed the road safely. It was so unfortunate on this day as there were no military personnel to help regulate the traffic. It was a struggle to cross the road since drivers hardly obeyed traffic regulations then. There was a close neighbor of ours whose children attended the same school. I held the girl's hand, and my sister held her brother's hand to cross the road. Seeing a speeding trailer while crossing the road, I instantly fell unconscious. I can't really recall if the trailer hit us, but I know fear can do a lot and I feel I became unconscious because of what I thought was going to happen. The next thing I remember was being in a car with the girl I held hands with while crossing the road. I noticed other people in the car with us as we headed towards my school hospital. Seeing my sister roll on the ground and cry hysterically made me so emotional as I could tell how she felt about the situation. I could assume she was so uncertain of whether her only sister would survive or not. It was literally the first time I consciously felt more pain than I could bear.

I saw my mom cry and sing the song "Giving Glory to the Lord, He Reign". Any day this song runs through my mind, I tear up. I saw the startled faces of my other siblings when they returned and found me in a condition that they weren't expecting. They couldn't believe what happened to their baby sister. So many neighbors came to visit after we returned from the hospital and extended their sympathy.

I dislocated my wrist, had an injury that almost made me blind, and had bruises all over my body. After some basic treatment, we were directed to a hospital that was better equipped. The next day, looking pitied with my bandage, we headed to the hospital. In the hospital, I saw a lot of people with amputated hands and legs. I thought to myself, that would have been me, but God saved me. It was more reason to thank God that the accident happened the way it did. The enemy might have planned way worse, but God showed up.

During my recovery, I had to go to a massage therapist daily. At one point my wrist had gotten better, then it went back to hurting. I had to change massage therapists over three times just to see if my wrist could get better. It took years to get things back to normal. This time was such a hard season for me, coupled with the fact that I was very young. I had people pity me, unnecessarily, which made me even more sad with my situation.

The memories of that day were still vivid for years. I began to fear the outcome of life because I would've never imagined what I was dealing with at age seven. I heard a lot of people say as you grow older, you continue to face more challenges. This got into my head and made me begin to fear the future. I had so many thoughts about what could happen to me in the future if I'm already dealing with so much from age seven.

My physical wounds took time to heal as it was so difficult to get my wrist back to normal. It was my right wrist, so I struggled with writing and doing things in my daily life. People helped me write in school and carry my things. I basically couldn't do anything that required me to use my right hand for some time. When there was no one to help me write in school, I managed to use my left hand and that wasn't easy to handle since I'm not a lefty. I think the most difficult part as a child was watching my mates play and not being able to because my right hand might be smacked unknowingly.

After my physical recovery, I struggled with moving forward from the mental and emotional traumas I suffered as a victim of a car accident. I practically hated and became so afraid of moving cars that I found it hard to cross the road. Even when I was held by someone, I sometimes left the person in the middle of the road and ran back. It took so much courage to embark on trips, unless my dad was the one driving. The first time I traveled on a bus after the accident was in 2011. One of my Aunties had her wedding date approaching and my mom had to travel with my sister and me. When I found out we were using the bus, I almost refused to go. I was in the middle of thinking 'What if the bus gets involved in an accident' and 'What will I miss if I don't travel for my Aunt's wedding?' I found the courage to go with them but what happened made me think of how I will return home with the same route. On the way, we got to a place with very terrible roads. The bus was trying to find its way out as the roads were not leveled and I screamed when it looked like the bus was going to fall. People laughed at my reaction, but I couldn't find the humor in my trauma. I became so ashamed when people laughed and thought 'If only they knew what I was dealing with they probably would have just kept quiet'. The trauma of being a victim of a car accident was a real thorn in my side and a huge part of the fears I began to have for life.

Traumas are strongholds that can limit you from moving forward. Sometimes we don't know how it indirectly affects other areas of our lives. I couldn't tell how a car accident affected how I viewed my future and life in general. Sometimes the experience we deal with after we come out of situations can get so real, like the incident, but I want you to know that the God you serve is more real than whatever experience you might have had. Fear gripped me so hard until 2022. It felt like this incident was playing a huge role, negatively, in some areas of my life and I knew I had to get to the root of it and partner with God to deal with it.

Our God is a healer, and He is able to heal you from any trauma you're going through. I want you to spend some time getting to the root of the problem. Think of what happened in your childhood. Decide to heal and move forward. It takes just your faith and trust in God all through the process. You are coming out strong!

Death-The Other Path
There is a path people go through and never live to tell how it looks. The path of death is a path we will all walk someday, but we pray we don't die untimely. On September 24th, 2018, I remember so well-as well as I know my name, the real enemy planned to take my life and it almost looked like his plans were coming to pass but guess what? God showed up!

The enemy's job is to steal, kill and destroy but we can't allow him to have his way. I was terribly ill, and I passed out twice before I was rushed to the hospital. That was the first time I was admitted to the hospital. Before then, I had been receiving home treatment. I had a nurse put me on a drip at home just to see if I could get better. It wasn't progressing, so the drip was removed halfway.

It was a Monday night after the drip was halfway removed, I remember telling my mom to help me get to the restroom. The last thing I remembered before I passed out was my mom screaming the name JESUS. When I began to regain consciousness, I heard the voices of people praying in my house. I was so surprised to see people whom I know live quite a distance from my house. It made me wonder how they were able to get to my house within the few seconds I thought I stayed unconscious, only for my sister to tell me how I've been lying lifeless for more than fifteen (15) minutes.

I had a glimpse of death and saw myself walking through a very dark path. I'm not sure who or what I saw but I know I met the mercies of God that brought me back to life. I heard the voices of people praying as I began to speak in tongues while regaining consciousness. As they continued praying, I heard them telling me to keep speaking. A glimpse of my experience that I was able to notice looked like what I've seen in movies, and I couldn't believe what God did in my life that day.

After I fully regained consciousness, we decided to go to the hospital. My mom packed some items I needed since I was going to be admitted. On our way, we discovered the road to the hospital was blocked because it was being repaired. We had to return home hoping that I would be better, and we could find our way to the hospital the next day since it was already 10:00pm. Coming down from the car and going into the house, I passed out again. Immediately, we had to find our way to another hospital. I was rushed to the emergency room at 11:00pm and was put on a drip that would last until the next day. My parents stayed overnight with me in the hospital while my sister had to stay the night at our cousin's house. The next morning, I had some tests done. The results displayed my diagnosis of malaria and typhoid. The days I spent in the hospital made me realize how good health is such a blessing. Sometimes we complain so much about 'little' things like not having the best car or living in the best place, but we don't realize how blessed we are to be in good health. After three days in the hospital with a lot of medication, I was discharged and given some medication to take home and it lasted for about a month. I was told to return for checkups the following month. On my next checkup, I was prescribed another set of drugs that lasted three weeks. I grew up disliking medication and it was really hard to take tablets. I could literally spend up to an hour trying to take tablets because it irritates me. This made it so hard for me to tell my parents when I got sick. I would always wait until they figured it out themselves. After this experience, no one would ever remind me to tell them when I feel even slightly sick.

Truly, I walked through the valley of the shadow of death, but God was with me. What God did in my life is difficult to put into words. If there was something I learned from this experience it was that God never leaves us. You might be walking through the dark part of your life right now, but I want you to know that God is with you. He already said He will never leave nor forsake you. He will be with you till the very end of the earth.

There was a season in my life when I got sick frequently, probably around the end of high school. It got to a time when my brother told me to recheck my genotype. My genotype is AA, but it didn't seem like it in that season. I struggled so much with sicknesses that I feared going to college. Even during my application process, there was a day I became so sick and feeling feverish that I was rushed back home. Some weeks before my JAMB (an exam we take in Nigeria before getting into college) I felt so sick that it was hard to study. Everything that was happening at that time was so crazy, but one thing is that God teaches me through everything I experience. I believe so much in the healing power of God not just because I have seen Him heal others, but because I have received healing even in my worst pain.

The sickness you may be going through, though it looks like it is unto death, is for the glory of God. Jesus told Mary and Martha that Lazarus' sickness was not unto death but for the glory of God. Jesus kept saying that Lazarus was not dead but sleeping. That was so hard to believe because Lazarus had been dead for four days. God wants to glorify himself through that pain. People need to see that God is good and you also need to experience the goodness of God in your life. You are not forgotten by God. He sees you and your healing is here!

Sick of Anemia

I have been highlighting very profound experiences of my life that God brought me out of. I can't fail to talk about 2021 which was such a hard year for me. In April, I fell terribly ill with anemia and my blood percentage was as low as 35%. I had a fast heart rate, shortness of breath, and weakness.

It was during my college examination period and my sight was badly affected which made it uneasy to study well. I was in my first year (second semester) at Rivers State University, Nigeria. College life was hectic. The workload can be so much and getting sick in school can be terrifying. I was so grateful to God that this happened at the end of the semester, and I could focus on my treatment during the holiday. I packed my bag the day before my last examination and was ready to leave for home immediately after my papers were completed. After experiencing my health issues in 2018, I stopped hesitating when it came to telling my parents when I felt sick, so I called them to let them know I was going to take a test when I returned. I got home and the next day, which was a Saturday morning, my nurse came home and took a sample of my blood for testing. Towards the evening of that same day, I was walking to church for choir rehearsals, when I met my nurse on the way. She asked where I was going, and I told her I was headed to church for rehearsal. Her response was:

"Well, Rejoice if you knew what was wrong with you now, you probably would have been resting." I promise you, my heart skipped as I wondered what would have been wrong with me. As we climbed the stairs she asked if my parents were around, and I said yes. I was still trying to figure out what was really wrong. When she told us my blood percentage was just 35% and I needed a blood transfusion, the enemy kept whispering that I was going to die.

The nurse, I call her a nurse of Faith, decided to take care of the issue without having me go for a blood transfusion. I was injected sixteen (16) times over a week and had to be on medication for over a month. This season was one of the most difficult seasons of my life. It was a time I had no option but to trust God. I knew no one could save me but God.

Still dealing with the illness, I had so many attacks spiritually which gave room for fear to come in. I couldn't stay in the dark, found it difficult to sleep alone, and had so many ugly unreal thoughts and nightmares. For over a year, my peace was stolen. I couldn't even have a good night's rest except when someone slept with me. Dealing with fear was such a hard journey. It came to a point when I had to ask God why He was allowing me to go through this 'situation abuse' at a young age. I called it 'situation abuse' because I was too young for what came my way. What I never understood was that God does not waste our pain. I never knew God was using this season of my life to grow my faith in Him. I believe God wanted to use this season to expose **me** to me. It was in this season I realized I had been living in fear for years and I needed to deal with it. I did so much just to get out of the situation. I cried so many times. My journal was filled with "God please help me overcome". When I go through my journal today, I am just so thankful. This was my journal entry on September 19th, 2021-

"Dear Lord, I must be honest. I have gotten weary in praying against the spirit of fear. I pray that you revive my faith in you and reactivate my prayer life. Amen."

God is so good and international about our lives. He never allows us to go through anything in vain. One thing we need to know is that God will never allow us to go through anything without birthing the glory.

"I consider that our present sufferings are not worth comparing with the glory that will be revealed in us."
Romans 8:18 NIV

This scripture is so real to me. It is one of my favorite scriptures because I have experienced it, and I still hope for tomorrow's glory. Whenever I go through anything, no matter how tough, the Holy Spirit directs me to that scripture. It gives me so much hope to know that what I'm going through is part of the plan for the glory that is yet to come.

That season of my life is the reason you can read this book today. I never in my life thought of writing a book. The day God told me "You're not coming out of this fire empty" and that He has given me a book to write, was so funny to me because I never knew anything about writing a book. I was just like "God, you can tell me to share my story through speaking but writing? Nah." I didn't think I could write well. I remember reaching out to my mentor after one of her Zoom meetings that spoke to me. I told her how God has given me a book to write and I'm not sure I write well. She said, "You don't have to be a good writer, just write. You are a best-selling author. Your story is someone else's deliverance. I can't wait to read your book." This gave me so much confidence to start writing regardless of how inadequate I felt. Today, I can look back and rejoice because what the enemy meant for evil, God turned it around for good.

Hey, you have all it takes to overcome. You have Jesus and He already overcame. It is my hope that you realize that regardless of what you're going through, you can come out strong. It's time to take your shield of Faith and defeat the enemy.

CHAPTER TWO: THE HEALING JOURNEY

"I have realized that God has the power to heal you instantly but sometimes He wants you to go through that process so that you can become a solutionist."

Healing is a journey and a process that might take time. I have come to realize that we all have a different healing journey which doesn't always happen in the time that we expect it to. The best partner to walk you through your healing journey is God because true healing comes from Him. The road to healing is not always smooth. It can get rocky, but God is too good to let you go through it alone. In your journey to healing, you must continue to strive to finish strong and get through no matter how rough the road may be. Every sickness and trial I went through took time to heal physically, mentally, and otherwise.

First, you need to realize that healing is possible, and it comes from God. I can definitely understand how some pain may seem impossible to heal from and at that moment we can decide to act on our feelings. We may not realize how it affects others or maybe we just try to blame our actions on what we went through or the people that caused us pain. This world would be better if people decided to take responsibility for their healing. I have heard people accept to be who their pain caused them to be without thinking of how it affects others. We continue to repeat circles when we do not decide to let the negativity end with us. When I see people behave a certain way, I think of how that baton of pain was passed to them. When we don't heal, we pass the negativity to those around us and even to our children. We must decide to end the cycle of pain so those who come after us do not have to battle the same cycle but will experience the healed version of us. Maybe you were sexually abused, bullied, or left heartbroken. You deserve to be healed.

When I was in the process of healing from the traumatic accident, I complained a lot and my mom always told me to ask God for healing. I think that shaped me so much in my relationship with God as I grew up knowing that I can talk to God about any of my situations. The journey to my physical healing from the accident wasn't an easy journey, as I couldn't do well what I would normally do with my hand. Aside from the physical healing, it took over 13 years to heal from it mentally and emotionally. Most of the time we think healing is impossible because of how long it takes but God is saying "delay is not denial". What's important is to accept the journey and trust God in the process. Healing is made available as it is the bread of God's children. It is God's will to see that we heal from everything holding us bound.

The truth is that God does not just want to heal our physical bodies, but he also cares about our emotional and mental state. Healing is available to us believers through the activation of our faith in God. In scripture, we see Jesus do a lot of miracles healing the infirmities of people. God loves us so much that he does not want us to remain in pain. This is why he has made healing available. He desires to heal every aspect of our lives, but we must embrace the journey of healing.

Jesus was touched by people's circumstances and had compassion for them. The healing power demonstrated by Jesus gave glory to the Father. God still wants to receive the glory through that situation you may be passing through, so he desires your healing much more than you do. No one was deprived of healing in scripture so long as they had faith and believed that they could be healed by Jesus. Healing may not happen instantly because God always does things in his timing.

In 2019, I was given an injection in the wrong direction which immediately made me paralyzed. It took some days before I could properly walk again. It's been over four years, and I can't say that my left leg has gone back to normal, but I can say that I am totally dependent on God in this journey. As much as I still believe in God for total healing, I am still thankful for the healing process.

At some point in 2023, I started having high symptoms of neuropathy and difficulty in mobility in my left leg. I went for a test and after I received my results, I was told to come back for an X-ray. I almost got depressed because I never saw this season coming. I did an X-ray and got my result, and it stated that I have a spiking in my tibial spines. I remember asking God again why He has to let me go through this season at this age. I was struck by His response. God told me that the glory that is to come is also not a respecter of age. There are days I cry my eyes out asking God why it has to be me and why the healing I need is taking longer. Regardless of everything, God's track record of healing me in the past has become a constant reminder that this too will pass. I'm not moved by this present moment. I'm just so sorry for the devil who's wasting his time because when glory comes, there will be no words to say.

I have realized that God has the power to heal you instantly but sometimes He wants you to go through that process so that you can become a solutionist. God doesn't just want to heal you; He wants to make you a vessel through which He can heal others. Oh, do you think God is allowing you to go through that process for nothing? No. In that process, He is making you and building you to not just be healed but to be able to bring healing to others.

One characteristic of a good leader God portrays, which I've come to realize, is that He is interested in our growth to become more like Him, than giving us all we need at a blow. A good leader wants to raise leaders who can lead others. This was while Jesus lived all His life on earth portraying what we have been given authority to do. Jesus told His disciples that everything they see Him do, they can also do.

"Very truly I tell you, whoever believes in me will do the

works I have been doing, and they will do even greater things than these because I am going to the Father."
John 14:12 NIV

So, when we have this in mind, we are reminded that God is birthing something out of the pain we are presently going through. Healing is a journey and some journeys take longer than others. It can get hard but I'm assuring you that all you have to do is trust God in this process. It took the woman with the issue of blood twelve years before she was made whole. How about the man at the pool of Bethesda? It took him thirty-eight years to be healed. These Bible stories are stories of hope to anyone believing in God for healing.

I had a healing conversation with some young believers, and we were discussing why some people do not receive healing when they ask for it. Basically, a guy asked why people pray for healing for years without receiving it. These were my responses: I think some reasons people don't get healing when they pray for it is:

- God's Timing: It might not be God's time yet. God's timing is perfect, and he does his things at the right time. Sometimes we trust God for something but don't trust when he will do it. It is important to not just trust God but to also trust his timing. It can get frustrating when we pray for something, and it isn't forthcoming, but we need to know that God is right on time. It can be scary to know that God's timing for healing can also be when we transition into eternal life. Some people will get their healing through physical death. The word of God made us understand that in heaven, there shall be no more pain, sorrow, sickness, etc. In this situation, we receive grace to bear the sickness until we meet our Father in heaven. Sometimes, the perfect healing we truly need (not want), happens when we go home, to Heaven, to rest. When we live with eternity in view, we will understand this. It can be scary, but it is the truth.

- Disbelief: This is another thing I think hinders healing. Matthew 21:22 says *"If you believe, you will receive whatever you ask for in prayer."* Sometimes, we pray and still doubt ourselves. God wants us to have so much confidence in who He is and what He can do in our lives. Nothing is impossible with God. It takes our faith in Him to change our situations.

- Disobedience: The last thing I pointed out is disobedience to God's direction. It is important to note that the healing power of God is directional. God will sometimes give us instructions to activate our healing. God heals in different ways. He is not a one-way traffic God. He works in different ways. In scripture, we see that some healing happened by the laying of hands, and some happened by just commanding the sickness to leave. Jesus also had to spit on the ground, make some mud with the saliva, and rub on the eyes of the blind man for him to see, some people had to go to the pool to get healed. Has God directed you to do something to be healed? Maybe it was to take that medication or maybe book a therapy session or whatever it may be. What's stopping you? How much do we listen for instructions when we pray for healing?

God is ever ready to heal us, but we have a part to play. When you pray, how much more do you believe? How well are you listening to God for directions in order to get healed? How much more do you trust God's timing? I want you to ponder these questions. My hope for you is that you embrace the journey of healing the Lord has set before you. Healing is your destination, and you will surely get there.

I have experienced, in many ways, the Healing Power of God through Faith that no one can convince me that God isn't real. I may not see Him, but I believe, and He works for me. When we go through situations that look like the path of death, God is still right there with us. He already said He will be with us and will never leave. His words are "Yes" and "Amen". If I was brought back to life, I want you to believe that God can also do the same in your life. It may not be the same situation. It could just be things in your life that need to come back alive. Can you boast about your Faith so much that it overrides your fear? Can you activate your Faith button and deactivate the button of fear? God wants you to just believe.

There is so much pain going on in the world right now. So many people are broken. It takes total surrender and faith in God to go through these times. The truth is, that God has already equipped you for whatever healing journey he wants you to embrace. Is it a journey of five years? Or three years? Regardless of how long or short it is, you are clothed with the full armor of Christ to win.

I have had different healing journeys for different sicknesses. The journey wasn't the same. For some sicknesses I got instant healing, for some, I had to undergo medical treatments, for other, I had to believe in God for years. The most important thing was how I didn't just get healed in that journey, but my faith was also made stronger. Today, I trust God more when I go through whatever sickness because if He did it before, He can do it again. God has a track record of keeping His word and He's not about to stop doing it now.

Are you believing in God for healing today? It may be physical, mental, emotional, or even spiritual. I want you to embrace whatever journey it comes with and trust that God is walking with you. I pray that you don't just get healed, but that God works on your heart and uses your one goal - to get healed, to accomplish more in your life. I promise this too will pass. You will look back one day and be grateful for God's faithfulness.

3 CHAPTER THREE: PANICKING SOLVES NOTHING

"We can either panic in situations or see the situation as a medium to be courageous."

When you're in a tough situation, panicking is the worst way to respond. The enemy adds more complication to our original problem by letting us panic. Now, let's have an honest conversation. Think of a moment when you panicked in hard times, what did it yield? Yeah, I know, it got worse. When we go through rough seasons in our lives, God wants us to turn to Him. He is the God of peace. I would advise you to try Jesus instead of panicking. I've had a series of panic attacks and in those moments, what actually made me feel better was turning to Jesus. I would play some worship music, write out the thoughts I get when I panic, and give it all to God in prayers. Laying down everything at the feet of Jesus is what is required of us when we experience things that should cause us to panic.

I can't recall any good that has ever happened when I panicked in trying times. Think about the disciples while traveling to the other side of the sea with Jesus. When the storm came, they panicked, and nothing changed until they acknowledged the presence of Jesus who is the Prince of Peace. Listen, Jesus said, "Peace be still". "Still" meaning to remain/not change. This shows that there was peace in the boat already; the disciples just needed to come to the knowledge that Jesus was all the peace they needed. I had panic attacks for years that disrupted my peace. I feared little things and anticipated negativity. I always had the "what if" thought and it was so noticeable that a lot of people always said, "Rejoice, you fear too much".

I always had the excuse of being careful, but it wasn't just carefulness, it was fear. Peace is not just a state of tranquility, but it can also mean a state of rest even in trouble. A lot of us never realize that we have Jesus, the Prince of Peace, inside of us which is why we are too quick to get troubled in situations. Feeling peaceful is not just being without trouble, but it means looking beyond the troubles around you and resting in God's arms. The Bible says in John 14:1 *"Do not let your hearts be troubled. Believe in God and believe also in me"*. Jesus is all the Peace you need! Fear is never from God; it comes from believing the wrong way. Faith is believing in God and everything He can do. Fear, on the other hand, is believing in what the devil can do and the harm he brings. The Bible says in 2 Timothy 1:7 *"For God has not given us the spirit of fear; but of power, and of love, and of a sound mind"*. Fear is a spirit; therefore, we have to fight it, not with physical weapons, but with the weapons of our warfare which is the full armor of God.

In Job 3:25, Job said, *"The thing which I greatly feared is come upon me and that which I was afraid of is come unto me"* When we fear, we anticipate what the enemy is about to do. The devil gets the full permission to harm us when we become so fearful that we forget what our God is and what He can do. I think we all have to come to the point of viewing God as truly our shepherd. And, because you have a shepherd that created everything on earth, a shepherd that has every power in Him, a shepherd whose eyes are always watching over you, then no evil can harm you.

To anticipate means to expect something, and one thing about the enemy is that he runs with our expectations. Fear is an invitation for the devil and what he has to offer and there is nothing good about what the enemy gives. It's either sickness, issues with your finances, death, etc. The enemy only comes to steal from you, kill, and destroy you. As Christians, we can either decide to let him steal from us or respond with our faith in God. Our faith in God is positively powerful while fear is negatively powerful. That means that they both are actively at work depending on which we choose to be at work in our lives. So, it is time to choose which to activate and it's time to redirect our belief, holding on to the faith we have received. I don't know about you but I'm choosing to activate my Faith in God. I don't care how little, but we have a God that moves mountains and breaks chains just with a little faith.

The devil is so passionate in attacking how we believe and what we believe in. He acts on our beliefs. Think about how many times you have partnered with the enemy in one situation or another through your belief. Think about how you have unknowingly given the enemy an invitation through your thoughts. The devil moves back and forth seeking for whom to devour. He won't get in unless he finds an available space. Fear makes room for the availability of the devil and the only way to close that availability is to stand firm and fight that spirit of fear. When it gives a knock at the door of your heart, you respond by showing that you've got faith already and there's no space for fear to come in.

One thing that fear does is stop us from stepping into the calling God has for our lives. I struggled while stepping into the calling God has for me because I wasn't sure I was capable of handling it. But the truth is that we are not the ones to handle the calling God has for us. All we have to do is obey His instructions and allow Him to take us through accomplishing the assignments He has given to us. Life is full of uncertainties, and it is almost a norm to fear and panic about the outcome.

There is something called "Fear of the unknown". It is the tendency to be afraid when you have no idea or information about something you face. We can either panic in situations or see the situation as a medium to be courageous. Think about the story of Joshua and Caleb in the Bible. Out of the twelve spies sent to Canaan, they chose to be positive regardless of what they saw because they knew the God they served. When we view things with fear, we doubt the ability God has put in us. It was the trust they had in God that made them see things differently. Others saw giants and were afraid, but they saw the giants and remembered their God is greater. When life gets uncertain we are expected to run to our creator who is certain about our lives. You are created to overcome everything life brings because He that is in you, is greater than he that is in the world. You've got the victory through Jesus.

Maybe you've been so afraid of starting that business or acting on that idea God has given to you. Some of us might have missed opportunities because of fear but it's so beautiful that we have a God that restores. You need to know you have a reason not to panic-God. If God has sent you into that room, walk in like God sent you! If God gave you the business ideas, start that business as God told you to do so!

Fear is such a big hindrance and limitation to our progress in life. Sometimes we think we don't have enough to move forward or that we are not good enough. I wrote this book with you in mind. I feel you and I understand how it can be. I have been there, I lived in fear for so long. As far as I can remember, it took thirteen (13) years to break free. Breaking free does not mean things don't come back to haunt you, but it does mean that you are now even more equipped to strategically fight and claim the victory that Jesus already won. God is more than able to provide for that business, ministry, schooling, etc. If he has told you to do something, know that he has already equipped you for it and he will provide all you need. God wants us to always trust him in the midst of uncertainties instead of panicking.

During my application process into college in 2019, it came to a time when I panicked a lot. Even if I got admitted, there was a chance I would miss attending college because of my finances. My parents and siblings tried to keep me calm and encourage me to rewrite the exams and reapply the next year. I felt it was way better if I didn't get accepted than getting accepted and not having the funds to attend. I saw "Admission in progress" in my portal, which means I would get admitted soon. I didn't know how to feel if I were told I wouldn't get into school that year. I panicked so much and had so many weird thoughts of things I could do to make sure I got into college. I really forgot what God can do and I rely so much on my thoughts and how bad the situation was.

One night, I took a picture of myself crying and sent it to my siblings telling them how I felt about the whole situation. Of course, siblings will be siblings. They thought I was just being too dramatic. I cried to my siblings, but I forgot I could cry to God and talk to Him about it. That same night I decided to talk to God about everything and how I felt. Prior to this time, I already had plans of not doing the "Jesus thing" on campus. I literally had plans of how I was going to live a life that didn't please God. Sometimes we don't get what we need because of our wrong motives. At that point, I had to reevaluate and this time around, it was directed towards pleasing God. I made a promise to God that night that I would make him known in college through my lifestyle if He made a way for my schooling. I had started journaling at that time, so I wrote in my journal

"LORD, I TRUST YOU AND I KNOW THAT NOT EVEN FINANCES CAN STOP ME FROM GETTING INTO COLLEGE THIS YEAR".

When I look back, I see God's goodness. When I think of how God has shown up for me countless times, that becomes a reason to not panic. If God did it before, He can do it again. He serves as a promise keeper and a way-maker. God made a way for me. I got into college, and I graduated four years later. I am so thankful that I trusted God in that season of my life, and he showed up.

The Bible says "So do not fear, for I am with you, do not be dismayed, for I am your God. I will strengthen you and help you. I will uphold you with my righteous right hand". Isaiah 41:10.

There came a point in my life where I struggled with panic attacks for a whole week. I had a terrible dream which made me start overthinking. It was hard to sleep at night as I felt so uneasy. One day, I preached in my ladies' community on a topic titled 'A Path to Eternity.' That night, I had crazy thoughts of not seeing the next day. I kept thinking 'Oh, what if people start posting my pictures with "RIP" on them, explaining how I had just preached on eternity and have transitioned into that path.' The devil is so determined that he can even use the scripture to make us think amidst. As my panic attacks got worse that night, I had to call my parents and have them pray for me over the phone. One of the statements my mom made was 'You always preach to others and encourage them, it's time to speak against the enemy's attacks.' I reached out to my sisters in Christ to cover me up in prayers. It was on the Sunday of the same week that I got to church and one of my prayers was 'God, every panic attack ends here in your presence.' It was there and then I got my healing.

The next time anxiety tries to have you, remember who and whose you are. You are a child of the most high King who never leaves nor forsakes his children. Remember you have a God upholding you with his right hand. Therefore, no evil can befall you.

Fear not! Everything will work out in your favor.
Fear not! Your business will flourish.
Fear not! Your ministry will grow and bless many lives.

Fear not! You will succeed.

Fear not! God is providing more than enough to pay your bills.

Fear not! You got this because God got you.

CHAPTER FOUR:
THERE IS POWER
IN THE NAME
OF JESUS

"When you call someone by their name, you invite their presence. Calling the name of Jesus invites his presence to the scene He is being called to."

I don't know if you already know this but I'm here to remind you just in case you have forgotten-THERE IS POWER IN THE NAME OF JESUS! The name of Jesus is able to save in the time of trouble. The Bible says in Psalms 50:15 *"Call on me on the day of trouble; I will deliver you and you shall glorify me."* The name of Jesus is the only name that can save and deliver you from fear. If death couldn't hold Him captive, then fear doesn't stand a chance. God is saying *"Fear not for I am with you"*. When we realize we can call on the name Jesus, the name that makes principalities and power bow, the name that makes sicknesses and diseases run, then we won't be moved by anything that comes our way. At the mention of the name of Jesus, every knee shall bow, and every tongue shall confess that Jesus is Lord. His name is that strong tower that the righteous run to and are saved.

The name of Jesus sets us free from any captivity of the enemy. The Bible says in Acts 4:12 *"Neither is there salvation in any other: for there is no other name under heaven given among men, whereby we must be saved"*. The name "Jesus" means savior and He is the whole reason for our existence. He died so that we may live. While we were yet sinners, he came and saved us, giving us the freedom that we needed. Listen, you have a savior, a helper who you can run to and be healed, delivered, and freed from any stronghold of the enemy. When we come to the understanding of the name of Jesus, we fear no evil. A lot of us scream the name of Jesus almost every moment but have not come to the realization of the power in His name. Miracles happen in the name of Jesus. Generational curses are broken in the name of Jesus.

Philippians 2:9-11 says "Wherefore God also hath highly exalted him, and given him a name which is above every other name: That at the name of Jesus, every knee should bow, of things in heaven and things in earth, and things under the earth;

And that every tongue shall confess that Jesus Christ is Lord, to the glory of God the father".

Jesus is Lord. He has authority over any and everything. If He is Lord over your life, then He has the authority and is more powerful than anything that tries to pull you down. When we receive Jesus, we accept Him not just as our savior but as our Lord, which means that He is the master of our lives. One incredible thing about having Jesus as the master of your life is that He is a master who has your best interest at heart. He is someone who wants to see you made whole and totally free from the bondage He already brought you out of. His name is above everything imaginable. Jesus is bigger than the challenges you are facing. He is Yahweh - He who Brings into Existence Whatever Exists. Jesus is the solution you need. In his name, chains of bondage break. The bondage of fear, sickness, and insecurities is lost.

When you call someone by their name, you invite their presence. Calling the name of Jesus invites his presence to the scene He is being called to. So, when we face fear, we have an advantage-Jesus, and we cannot overcome or win the battle without Him. We have to invite this name into any and every battle we face, permitting Him to fight for us. One thing about this master is that He gives you the will to choose. Are you ready to truly bring Him into every aspect of your life to take control.? A name is a spirit. We see in scripture how God had to change the name of some people in order for them to become who He wants them to be. When we talk about the name of Jesus it doesn't mean the pronunciation but "WHO" He is. God has highly exalted the name of His son. It's time to speak, walk, and act in that name.

Growing up, for those of us who had spiritually inclined parents, we were taught or somehow acquired from home culture to call the name of Jesus when we are hurt. Maybe it wasn't your parents but your Sunday school teachers or Pastors. Somehow, just maybe we never really knew how we were saved from trouble when we called the name Jesus but we saw it worked and we made it a continuous act to always call this name. The truth about the name of Jesus is that it is so powerful that it answers even when the person calling the name does not really have a full knowledge of why the name is being called. This is a name that people call even when they get into trouble, even when they have caused it themselves. This name has been so highly exalted by God that even people who have not accepted Jesus into their lives scream for help in the name because subconsciously, they know who the real savior is. I pray that we really get to understand the advantage we have as children of God that we refuse to allow the enemy's strategies to make us forget that we have Jesus and we can call on Him to be saved. The name Jesus is the most important name, and it is in this name we find our identity.

I preached to a guy some time ago and he asked me what our purpose on earth is. I told him that sometimes we focus more on knowing our purpose than we focus on knowing the God who gives the purpose. And the only way we know God is by accepting His son, Jesus. If you need something from someone, do you go ahead looking for the thing or the person that has what you need? You can never know who you have been created to be outside of Jesus. He is the way, the truth, and the life and you cannot reach God or know the plans He has for your life if you don't know His son. This means you cannot find life's direction outside of Jesus. You cannot know the truth which is the word of God outside Jesus and most importantly, you do not even have a life outside Jesus. He is everything you need in this life's journey. If you're still struggling to figure out how your life should look, then Jesus is all you need. You need to embrace Jesus and submit to Him. Accepting Jesus into your life as your Lord and Savior means that you are permitting Him to be in charge of your life, and that He ultimately stands to guide and save you from everything trying to get your soul.

We live in a generation where people are dependent on other things to get satisfaction. Young adults are getting into substance abuse, pornography, and other things detrimental to their lives. Some of these people need answers and guidance on how they can get out of their addictions. Many are afraid to reach out for help because of the shame that comes with it. If you are ever given the opportunity to have anyone reach out for help, the first thing I suggest you to do is lead them to Jesus. I strongly believe in therapy but therapy without Jesus changes nothing internally. It will take Jesus to get the best out of therapy. We need to stop bypassing the process to freedom and replacing it with a temporary alternative. The ultimate person these people need is Jesus before any other help. The ultimate solution you need to overcome fear, addictions, and insecurities is Jesus.

"And He said to them, "Go into all the world and preach the gospel to every creature. He who believes and is baptized will be saved, but he who does not believe will be condemned. And these signs will follow those who believe: In My name, they will cast out demons; they will speak with new tongues; they will take up serpents; and if they drink anything deadly, it will by no means hurt them; they will lay hands on the sick, and they will recover." Mark 16:15-18 NKJV

I want us to pay more attention to "In My Name". There is so much we can do in the name of Jesus. We defeat the enemy in the name of Jesus. Healing takes place in the name of Jesus.

Breakthrough happens in the name of Jesus. Your situation may seem impossible to change but listen, in the name of Jesus, everything bows, and chains breaks.

Acts 3:1-10 talks about a man who was lame from birth. He was kept at the temple gate called Beautiful. This man had lost hope that he would ever walk so he settled for less and had just enough money to feed himself. He never really realized that there was something in store for him more than money. See, sometimes we settle for less because we have lost hope for something better. This man needed Jesus more than he needed money. The money made him return to beg but what he truly needed more was for Jesus to heal him.

"Then Peter said, "Silver or gold I do not have, but what I do have I give you. In the name of Jesus Christ of Nazareth, walk."
Acts 3:6 NIV

I may not have money, but I have Jesus. I may not attend one of the best of schools, but I have Jesus. I may not live in a mansion, but I have Jesus. I may not be riding in a new model, car but I have Jesus. I may have no material thing, but I have something eternal. Material things fade away, but Jesus remains the same. I don't care what you don't have, but do you have Jesus? If you have Jesus, you have everything you need. If you have Jesus, then you have someone who controls everything. He brings to existence whatever exists. Your health may be declining, but the name of Jesus heals. Your marriage may be tearing apart, but the name of Jesus can restore. It's time to call that name and be free. It's time to renounce fear and pronounce faith in the name of Jesus.

5

CHAPTER FIVE: CONTROL YOUR THOUGHTS (THE MIND IS A BATTLEFIELD)

"Negative thoughts don't just stop coming when you decide not to think negatively but they stop when you replace them with positive thoughts."

The Bible says "As a man thinks in his heart, so is he." God already knows the power of how we think and what we think. The power in our thoughts is unimaginable, which is why we must strive to always think positively and in alignment with what God is saying over our lives. The mind is indeed a battlefield, so we need to be prepared to fight every thought that comes to destroy us. There are so many thoughts running in our mind day to day, both positive and negative. It takes a renewed mind through the word of God to overcome negative thoughts. Negative thoughts don't just stop coming when you decide not to think negatively but they stop when you replace them with positive thoughts. One aspect we sometimes fail to imply is replacing the negative thoughts we are letting go of with the positive ones. What I had running through my mind in the season where I experienced fear was what prompted the feeling of fear. For example, let's say I was on a relaxing trip and started having negative thoughts like wondering what would happen if the car's brakes malfunction and we got into an accident?' Just like I explained earlier, the trauma from the car accident I experienced still haunts my daily life. So, there have been many times when I've had negative thoughts, and my mind immediately flashed back to the experience I had when I was seven years old. One negative thought I've constantly had since 2021, especially at night, was the image of ugly beings appearing to me. I literally couldn't sleep peacefully for months because I had a fear of the unknown.

2 Corinthians 10:4-5 tells us that "the weapons of our warfare are not carnal but mighty through God to the pulling down of strong holds; Casting down imaginations and every high thing that exalts itself against the knowledge of God, and bringing into captivity every thought to the obedience of God".

The weapons we have as believers are not physical weapons but Spiritual. We win in the place of prayer and through the Word of God. Jesus's response, when tempted by Satan was "It is written". We overcome the devil by the knowledge we have of the Word of God. We need to know that we have a real enemy which is the devil, and he comes to steal, kill, and destroy. The devil might have stolen your faith and replaced it with fear, but it is time to take back your faith. One thing about the devil is that he is very interested in our thoughts, and he always starts by attacking our mind. Once he wins, he is able to do what he wants to do physically. When we think of something negative, we give the enemy an idea to run with. A lot of times he puts evil imagination in our minds, and we begin to see things that naturally aren't even real.

Fear means:

F- False
E- Experiences
A- Appearing
R- Real

The time I couldn't sleep alone wasn't because I saw anything physical, but it just kept running through my mind to the point it looked real. God wants us to be careful what we accept into our minds and strive always to hear what He is saying to us through His word. We have a place that we can always run to for the renewal of our minds-His Word. In order to keep your mind in the right state, you have to be consistent in renewing it. Remember, we wrestle not against flesh and blood but against principalities and powers. Therefore, we need something more than the natural to overcome them. We need God's Word which is spirit, life, and truth. God's Word is the armor we put on as believers. We use the words that we speak to fight, which is the Word of God.

The enemy has a way of putting thoughts of inadequacy or failure in the minds of believers that we sometimes forget what God says and what He can do. I studied the story of Gideon in the Bible, and I saw how fear can hinder us from even providing the solution that we need. Sometimes we complain so much about a situation without knowing we are the 'solutionist.' When Gideon asked in Judges 6:13: "Pardon me, my Lord, but if the Lord is with us, why has all this happened to us?", guess what the angel said to Gideon? He said "Go in thy strength and save Israel out of Midian's hand. Am I not sending you?" Gideon needed a solution to the problem without knowing he was the 'solutionist' to the problem. He had so many thoughts of inadequacy when he was told to go save Israel. Anytime I think of a problem around me and want to ask God why it is happening, I also think that maybe there should be a follow-up question-God, am I the one to bring a solution to this problem?'

I have come to realize that sometimes the person who cares so much to know the reason something is happening is most likely the person who is to bring a solution to that problem. The next time you get so burdened about what's happening in your family, place of work, or society, instead of just questioning why it is happening, ask God how He wants you to bring a solution to it.

The devil always tries to keep us bound by the thought of where we are coming from or who we think we are. One thing I have realized is that God does not call the qualified. It is those He calls that He empowers to be qualified. I love it when I think I can do nothing myself because that is the moment I get to acknowledge what God can do through me. I love it when I feel inadequate in my strength because that is when God's strength is made perfect in my weakness. Just like Gideon, you might have been wallowing in your thoughts, thinking that you aren't good enough or you don't have all it takes. I'm here to let you know that you have all you need to do what God has called you to do because God has already equipped you for it. God has not called you without equipping you. You have to stop defining yourself by your background, social status, or your bank account. Those are never criteria for God to use you.

In 2022, I was opportune to be featured as a contributing author in the BAM Magazine in Boston, Massachusetts. My article solely speaks on how young adults often do not realize who they are and what has been placed inside of them because they have been so caught up with societal accreditation. The beauty of being used by God is that He isn't interested in what you possess materially. God is more interested in what He has put inside of you. There is something God sees that we may not see until we look through His lens. The way we think as humans is very different from the way that God thinks.

"For my thoughts are not your thoughts, neither are your ways my ways, declares the Lord"
Isaiah 55:8

The way we think influences the way we live, either positively or negatively. You have to ask yourself these questions: Are my thoughts aligned with God's word? Does my thinking look like what God is saying about me? Controlling your thoughts should be an intentional day-to-day act. We have to guard our thoughts so much that we don't allow the enemy to tell lies to our mind. Limiting your beliefs is a negative trait that stops you from doing and becoming who you are meant to be. It may look like you just can't achieve anything, or you don't have what it takes, but sometimes it is just a mindset thing. Think about great people today. Some of them never had a rosy beginning. A lot of success stories I have heard sounded unrealistic because of how it is almost impossible to think something good could come out of their situations. These people did something remarkable which started from a change of mindset. They saw their situation as a push to do better rather than an excuse to be limited. There is so much we can achieve with a changed mindset. If you're a child of God, you have to think just like your Father, God, has designed you to think.

"Finally, brothers and sisters, whatever is true, whatever is noble, whatever is right, whatever is pure, whatever is lovely, whatever is admirable- If anything is excellent or praiseworthy- think about such things"
Philippians 4:8

Our minds need to be transformed daily not by what the world says but by what the Word of God says. I have trained myself with the help of the Holy Spirit not to think small and that has drastically changed me. Sometimes when I think of where I'm headed, my dreams, and where God is taking me, I lose sight of where I am currently. Not to say that I am not present in the moment, but I become aware that the present is just a moment. When you dwell on what you think, it becomes reality.

I don't know about you but I'm deciding to think and dwell on the promises of God. The best decision we can ever make when it comes to our mindset, is to think in alignment with God's Word and promises. If only we knew the plans God has for us, we would refuse to listen to the lies of the enemy. One thing about God is that He always unfolds (in bits) what He wants to do in our lives. We have one assignment for the fulfillment of His plans-to keep abiding. The things that God has in store for us are beyond our imaginations and sometimes we may not have the capacity to push through when it comes in full. This is why God requires that we consistently seek Him above all odds. He wants people who will say 'I will continue to seek you irrespective of the lies the enemy places in my mind.' Today, I'm encouraging you to keep abiding in God through His Word as He continues to renew your mind and unfold His plans for you.

"But as it is written: Eye has not seen, nor ear heard, Nor have entered into the heart of man The things which God has prepared for those who love Him."
I Corinthians 2:9 NKJV

The truth is that even the glimpse you can see of what God is working in your future is not compared to what He is doing. The devil was once close to God and knows how much greatness awaits the children of God. This is why he is striving to keep sending negative thoughts to your mind that do not align with God's thoughts. His goal is to keep you distracted from the blessings that are coming. You have to in return strive to guide your thoughts through the Word of God. You have to take control of what you think about as that will help you remove fear and live in faith.

CHAPTER SIX: GOD'S WORD IS THE ARMOR YOU NEED

"The Word is food for our spirit. If the Word of God is life, think of how much you're living or dying spiritually with how intentional you are with studying the Word."

Faith comes by hearing the Word of God. The Word of God is such a powerful tool we use to defeat the enemy. When fear arises, speak God's Word! Your enemy has an ear so open your mouth and speak. When the enemy comes with his lies, respond with the truth, which is God's Word. What the devil fights so much is our faith in God because he knows that your faith is your identity. The enemy brings situations that make you disbelieve what God can do. When you doubt someone's ability, it doesn't take long for you to start to doubt their existence. The enemy wants you to doubt that God exists, but we have a weapon to fight which is the Word of God. I did so many things to overcome fear. I fasted, prayed, and also studied God's Word. All these were helpful in the process, but the most effective tool was speaking God's Word over my situation.

The scriptures are not just mere written words, but they are living and active. The Word of God makes the enemy tremble. Haven't you noticed that it takes so much discipline to study the Word of God? The devil fights so hard to stop us from getting into the Word. The devil can start by making you struggle with being disciplined over little things, like the time you spend on social media, the time you spend watching movies, and even the time you spend with others on the phone. It can also be how you're not disciplined enough to eat well. Sometimes we overlook the little things but having discipline over those things affects the way we are disciplined enough to spend time in the Word. If we even go deeper, some of these things I have mentioned are hindrances to our ability to spend time with God's Word. I think prayer can be way easier than studying God's Word because you can pray while doing the dishes, driving, or even doing laundry but, studying the Bible effectively requires your undivided attention.

I struggled so much with studying the Bible and to be

honest, I sometimes still struggle but it's good to know that we have the Holy Spirit who is ever ready to help. You need to know that flipping through the pages of the Bible is different from studying. I like to make reference to the story of Martha and Mary when I talk about studying God's Word. Martha was so distracted while Mary chose what was better by sitting at the feet of Jesus to listen to the Word. One beautiful way that has worked for me in studying the Bible is approaching the Word of God with an "I don't know but am willing to learn" mindset. Could it be that Martha thought she already knew what Jesus was going to say, probably, because she had heard Him preach before?

I listened to a Pastor who said "Approaching the Word of God with an existing knowledge based on what you have read or heard before can hinder you from receiving a new revelation." I agree. Haven't you noticed that you could study a passage of the Bible again and again, and each time the Lord reveals something you never realized was in that exact passage? So, understanding the Word of God requires you to listen just as Mary did. The Bible always says "Hear ye the Word of the Lord." So, it's not about reading, it's about opening your ears to hear what God is saying and opening your heart to receive from Him. It's important to study your Bible every day. I understand the busyness of our lives can make us miss studying the Bible, but you can set reminders. The Word is food for our spirit. If the Word of God is life, think of how much you're living or dying spiritually with how intentional you are with studying the Word. The way we can't be healthy without the physical food we eat is the same way we are spiritually unhealthy without God's Word. We all need to know that the Word of God is God.

"In the beginning was the Word, and the Word was with God, and the Word was God."
John 1:1 NKJV

So, you aren't just reading a mere paper, you are studying a spirit-God, who is dynamic and can decide to reveal that which He wants to reveal. The extent to which you study the Word of God is the extent to which you know God. We are in a lost world where we hear a lot of wrong teachings and misinterpretations of the Word of God, but if we continue to study His Word, we can know what God is saying to us. We have Christians today who don't study the Bible but only listen to their pastor's sermons. Some people always say "My pastor said" which may not be wrong but what is God saying? In this kingdom, we survive only by the word of the one who created us, which is God. God's Word is the guidance we need to live in a world we do not belong to. There is so much noise in the world right now, but we can choose to redirect our ears to the Word of God.

Isaiah 55:11 says "So is my word that goes out from my mouth: it will not return to be empty but will accomplish what I desire and will achieve the purpose for which I sent it"

Every word spoken by God can never fail. If God says you're healed, delivered, and free, so is it! Apostle Paul told Timothy in 1 Timothy 4:13 "Until I come, devote yourself to the public reading of scripture, to preaching, and to teaching".

God wants us to get into His Word and eat. His word is strength. Jeremiah in scripture, ate God's words and was filled with joy. Everything you need to overcome is in the Word of God. The Word of God is quick and powerful. Speak it! Jesus spoke God's Word when He was tempted by the devil in the wilderness. After fasting for forty days and forty nights, the devil still had the audacity to tempt Jesus. The enemy is not scared of your prayers or how long you fast. The enemy is scared of what you know and stand on. When you know God's Word and stand firm on it, in the days of battle speak it forth!

Jesus spoke back with the Word of God, in the same way, we as children of God, should speak back to the devil. Take the sword of the spirit, which is the Word, and fight the enemy. If you're going through any situation, meet God right at His Word. John 4:47-53 tells us a story of a man who heard that Jesus was performing miracles. He had a son lying almost dead and he reached out to Jesus to come heal his son. Jesus said "Go, your son will live" and the man took Jesus at His Word. He returned home and saw that his son was made whole at that same moment Jesus had spoken. This scripture explains better how Jesus does not need to come down from heaven to heal or deliver us. He has already spoken His Word. It takes us to believe and hold onto.

There is a song by Don Moen titled "I Am The Lord That Healeth Thee" that explains how God's Word is enough to change things and make things happen. Take a moment and enjoy the words to the chorus below:
"I am the God
That healeth thee
I am the Lord
Your healer
I sent My word
And healed your disease
I am the Lord
Your healer"

Look at what it says, "I sent My word…" This means that for everything you need or everything you go through, you need His Word to get the Victory. Maybe, if the Bible didn't exist, that could have been an excuse, but we are not left without the Word of God.

Colossians 3:1 says "Let the word of Christ dwell in you richly". For every circumstance we find ourselves in, there is a word from God for it. One problem we have is that when we are in trouble, we check out other sources and only come to God when those sources don't work. God is saying, 'Your first response to any issue is to seek to hear Me and what I am saying about it' and not to go to the internet first. You just got diagnosed with an illness? Go to God and hear what His word says about healing instead of checking how many days you have to live because of the sickness. Your finances are not in a good state? Go to God and hear what His word says about provision. God has a word for everything you are going through.

The Bible is God's written words to you. Our Heavenly Father knew that this world would be noisy, and we needed to continually hear what He was saying to us. You're not left on earth without a word of guidance neither are you left without a Father who constantly seeks to communicate with you. When I hear people ask, "How do I hear God?", I ask how well are you listening? A lot of people are waiting to hear an audible voice calling their names, maybe just like Samuel in the Bible. They do not realize that God's word is right there with them.

I love that our God is so good to not restrict His voice to just be a sound. If it was so, how would the deaf people hear God? The Word of God is God Himself. Take note of the pronoun, the Word is realized to be a "He" and not an "It". Therefore, when you read God's Word, you read God. When you study God's Word, you study His lifestyle. This is why transformation happens through the Word of God. Do you think it is just the mere papers of the Bible that convicts you? No. God is a spirit, and the Word of God is God.

Like I said earlier, the enemy is afraid of the knowledge

you have of God through His word but most importantly, he is greatly afraid of when you walk in accordance with the Word. It is no joke that the Bible tells us to not just be hearers but also doers of the Word. It may surprise you to know that even the enemy is able to speak the Word back to you when you speak to him. As a believer, there should be a difference between you and the enemy when it comes to the Word of God. The difference is in the practice of the Word. The devil can speak the Word, but he can't practice the Word. We have to walk in accordance with what God is saying so that we do not just become people who know the Word but people who do what the word says.

I want to encourage you today to make the Word of God a lamp unto your feet and a light unto your path that you may be able to walk through even in the darkness of fear and shine your light. You have been given authority, use it! Use your God-given power to stop the devil from hanging around. When you know God's truth, you can't believe the lies of the enemy. We have to be so rooted in the truth that we are not moved by the lies of the enemy. Clothe yourself with your full armor and be ready to conquer!

"Take the helmet of salvation and the sword of the Spirit, which is the word of God."
Ephesians 6:17 NIV

The Bible verse above explains the Word of God to be the sword of the Spirit. Sword is a tool for fighting so this means that everything we need to fight the enemy is our sword which is the Word.

CHAPTER SEVEN: REST IN THE SHADOW OF HIS WINGS

"When life throws so much at you, it can make you depressed. Sometimes life will be out here "lifing" but we, as believers, have an advantage. We have a God who has already given us an open check to come to Him with all of our burdens."

When we go through challenging times, it can be a call to rest. Rest always proceeds your best.   When I was going through my moment of fear, I found out that God was calling me to rest in the shadow of His wings. Fear is always an anticipation of evil and knowing that God protects His own should give us courage instead of fear. But how can we get this courage if we don't rely on Him?

When we rest, we give God the chance to fight for us. His word in Exodus 14:14 says "The Lord will fight for you and you shall hold your peace". You can't fight this battle of fear alone. Therefore, God is the anchor and defender you need. All you need to do in the midst of a storm is rest. Be still and know who is there with you. Jesus resting in the boat during the storm is a footprint that we must follow as His followers. You have to be still and know that He is God. If Jesus rested during a storm, you need to follow in his footsteps and rest instead of worrying when you're faced with a storm. It is important to point out that resting is not a sign of laziness nor is it a sign of missing out. How many of you are workaholics? Sometimes I fall into this category and feel like I am lazy or I'm missing out whenever I decide to rest. Rest can be either physical, spiritual, emotional, or mental. Anyway, they are all important for our effectiveness. I struggled so much with resting and even now, I am still learning to be intentional with it. I can be such a night owl that sometimes I fight sleep when it comes way earlier than when I normally go to bed. I used to have this fear of missing out if I took out time to rest. I would just think of what work I could have finished with the time I'm using to rest. If our creator could take time to rest after creation, it is an example of how much we need rest to be effective. Think about it; we do not enjoy what we work for if there is no time to rest. When you rest, you're not missing out, instead, you are refilling and getting better for what is ahead. I have learned that if God is calling you to a place of rest, it is a time for preparation and equipping for the next level. When we go through fearful moments, it is a time to rest in God's presence. It is in God's presence that we find solace.

Talking about physical rest, I know you've got so many things to do but it is important to take out time to just be still in the presence of God. God's presence is the ultimate source of rest. I think that God's presence offers all of rest we need-physical, mental, or even emotional. We can always make His presence a priority before seeking out secondary aspects of rest which could be going on vacation, having a massage, etc. You can play worship music and just let the words sink down. When we are cumbered with a lot, it can hinder us from doing things right. Matthew 11:28-30 says "Come to me, all you who are weary and burdened, and I will give you rest. Take my yoke upon you and learn from me, for I am gentle and humble in heart, and you will find rest for your souls. For my yoke is easy and my burden is light".

When life throws so much at you, it can make you depressed. Sometimes life will be out here "lifing" but we, as believers, have an advantage. We have a God who has already given us an open check to come to Him with all of our burdens. Remember it's okay to feel so but what matters most is how you respond to it. God already knew we would get to a point where we feel so heavy so He already provided that safe space for us to receive the rest we need. Take a look at the story of Elijah in the Bible.

"...while he himself went on a day's journey into the wilderness. He came to a broom bush, sat down under it, and prayed that he might die. "I have had enough, Lord," he said. "Take my life; I am no better than my ancestors." Then he lay down under the bush and fell asleep. All at once an angel

touched him and said, "Get up and eat." He looked around, and there by his head was some bread baked over hot coals and a jar of water. He ate and drank and then lay down again. The angel of the Lord came back a second time and touched him and said, "Get up and eat, for the journey is too much for you." So he got up and ate and drank. Strengthened by that food, he traveled forty days and forty nights until he reached Horeb, the mountain of God."
1 Kings 19:4-8 NIV

Even Elijah went through a tough time when he fell into depression, which shows that as God's people, we are not exempted from our feelings of pain or depression but what's different is that we have a solution just right in front of us. Quitting has never been the remedy and is not the remedy to your problems. Elijah was weary but all he needed was to rest, eat, and be strengthened for the journey ahead. I hear God saying 'It is not over yet. Take some rest, eat, for the journey ahead is far and you need more strength to scale through.' A lot of you are carrying burdens that are to be laid at the feet of Jesus. Jesus paid for so much on the cross and He is still offering to help you carry those burdens. Sometimes, we struggle so much in life because we are trying to do that which only Christ can do for us. Jesus is saying today "Lay it at my feet". God's presence is a true source of rest for our hearts and souls. Resting in God's presence makes us approach work differently because we get refreshed for the next assignment. God wants us to find time even in our busy schedules to be in His presence. Get into His Word and communicate with Him. Remember communication is a two-way thing which means- that sending a message to God requires that you wait to hear back from Him.

Rest is powerful and it is a gift that God gives to His beloved. I like to think of the hen and her chicks as a little picture of what God does for us. Have you ever seen a hen cover her chicks with her wings when it's raining, and they are protected? It's just so beautiful to see that she prefers to be cold than for her chicks to be cold. This is how we are covered and untouched by the wind of life when we decide to find rest in God. Exodus 33:14 says, "The Lord replied, My presence will go with you and I will give you rest". God Himself rested on the seventh day after creation and He created our bodies to need rest. Rest is an expression of our trust in God. When we enter into our season of rest, it shows that we trust God enough to work things out even when it looks like we are not present at the moment

Accepting to follow Jesus changes everything in our lives as we have to give our all to Him and be rest assured that we are safe. You may have had your will, dreams, or things you have set out to accomplish but giving your life to Jesus means submitting all your dreams, will, and everything you set out to achieve. Rest sometimes looks like total surrender to God. The moment you surrender your life to Christ, your will, passion, goals, etc., also surrenders to him. Following Jesus is not always easy. Jesus said "Take up your cross and follow me" which means there is a cross to carry. The cross signifies death to self.

Life definitely happens to everyone and in those moments when you feel weary, it is a time to rest in the shadow of the almighty. Leaving your desires and deciding to follow the plan God has for you can be filled with so much fear and anxiety. To be honest, sometimes God's plan seems humanly impossible, and as humans, we are likely to feel overwhelmed. As much as God's future plans for us are beyond our imaginations, the process of getting there can be challenging.

I "unknowingly" started ministry at age of seventeen (17). That was in 2020. Don't be so surprised I said I started 'unknowingly'. The truth is that I obeyed God without knowing what it would look like. I always say "God has a way of getting His children. If I had known what I was getting into, I would have run from it. That day I decided to create a space for young ladies to be whole, I felt so much joy and I still feel so much joy seeing what God is doing with the ladies in my ministry. I've had so many dreams of where God is taking us, and it is so beautiful that God has so many amazing plans for us. I was so overwhelmed with joy that I didn't realize there would be a process. Listen, God is too good to take you somewhere he hasn't equipped you to stay. God is too good to give you something he hasn't trained you to handle. When I began facing challenges in ministry, I wondered if I was actually in my right senses when I made the decision to create a space for young ladies. At that time, I would have never imagined I would experience so many challenging moments. I thought 'Oh, if God called me for this, then, it will be all rosy'.

We need to know that the journey to greatness is not always easy and, in those moments, there is a tendency to give up. We often don't realize that the one who has called us has also made himself available for us to lean on. God knows exactly what we need, and He never withholds any good thing that is for us. God wants you to lay all those worries at his feet. Let your soul find rest in his embrace. You're God's little Princess/Prince and he desires to help you. It's time to trust God and cast your cares on him. This is not the time to lean on your own understanding. Your understanding has failed before and it will still fail you, but the love of God never fails. Leave your worries behind. It's time to sit at the feet of Jesus. His presence is the best place to be.

"Because you've been my help, therefore in the shadow of your wings I will rejoice"
Psalm 63:7

62

There is so much joy when we rest in the shadow of his wings. Rest is available for you today. Embrace the rest that Christ gives!

CHAPTER EIGHT: RELY ON GOD'S LOVE

"When we embrace the love of God, we begin to walk in the fruit of God's love as we become more like Him."

If we really knew how much God loves us, we would understand that nothing can harm us. When you're alone, on the highway driving, in your office, or in the dark, God is right there with you. David said, "Even if I walk through the valley of the shadows of death, I fear no evil for God is with me". This is the level of confidence we should have in Christ because we are not self-sufficient. We have a God who loves us so much that He saved us and gave us life. He portrayed this by sending His son to die for us. Regardless of where you are or what you walk through, God is with you, and nothing has the power to hurt you. Fear springs up from thinking something negative is about to happen. I want you to think about a God that sent His only son to die for you and me. We are the 'one' that Jesus left the 'ninety-nine' to chase after. If God could go that length, then He is able to save us from any trouble that life throws at us.

I attended a retreat in January of 2022. After one of the prayer sessions, I had a discussion with some other young people on how I have been dealing with fear. It was so crazy to hear almost everyone share similar experiences of how they have been battling with fear and that made me realize I wasn't alone. If we all can be sincere, we battle with fear at some point in our lives. I shared with these young believers how I sometimes couldn't mention or cast the enemy while praying because of fear. The devil knew and that was why he had so much authority over my mind. In that meeting, a guy shared with us how he sometimes feels fearful when he is alone in his room and immediately waves it off by saying "God loves me too much to let anything harm me". These words shifted my mindset and I began to see God's love differently. God's love for us didn't just end with what His son did on the cross. It is continuous and is made new every day.

It is one thing to know that someone loves you and it is another thing to feel the love someone has for you. Sometimes, we can't feel the love God has for us because we focus so much on our fears and insecurities. God wants us to redirect our focus today. Relying on God's love is so important, and it truly reflects on the way we love others. We can't fully love and serve others if we don't feel the love Christ has for us. 1 John 3:16 says "Hereby perceive we the love of God, because he laid down his life for us: and we ought to lay down our lives for the brethren". Sometimes when I find it hard to love others, I just think, maybe I am not loving myself enough to love others. And, not loving myself shows that I have refused to see myself the way God sees me. I will be truthful, loving some people can be hard but you have to see beyond what they have done to love them. In fact, sometimes I give more grace to people when I think of who I was and how it might have been difficult for people to love me. How about now? Maybe I still have some traits that make it difficult for some people to love me. I think seeing it this way lets us know that we are all imperfect humans. As children of God, we have to extend the love we have received from God to others. Indeed, you can't die for people just as Jesus did but, you can love people. I have struggled with loving people especially when I can clearly see that they don't have my best interest at heart. Sometimes, there is a fear that comes with trying to love people who have hurt you in the past or who clearly do not love you. In this moment, it is important to submit your heart to God, let go of fear, and show people the love that they may not even deserve - because guess what? Somehow, we aren't deserving of God's love but yet, He keeps showing us how much He loves us. When we realize that we were in one way or another not deserving of what Christ did on the cross for us, then we can give grace to others knowing that God also loves them regardless. Relying on God's love helps you see yourself the way God sees you and also see others as God sees them. You don't have to fear the outcome of extending God's love to those who don't even love you.

"There is no fear in love. But perfect love drives out fear because fear has to do with punishment. The one who fears is not made perfect in love."
1 John 4:18 NIV

God's love is perfect, and it drives out fear. There are so many insecurities we can overcome if we truly see ourselves through the lens of Christ. One of the ways I was able to overcome fear was by allowing the Holy Spirit to help me feel God's love. It can be hard to feel God's love in the midst of challenges, but we have our helper-The Holy Spirit. It's important that we constantly ask the Holy Spirit to reveal the love of God to us even when it looks like we are alone. Whenever I feel fearful, I just think of what Christ did for me on the cross of Calvary. It was not the nails that held Jesus on the cross, it was LOVE. If Jesus could pay the price I owe with His precious blood, then fear was part of what He paid for. My fears are drowned in perfect love, and I refuse to be a slave to the enemy.

..."so that Christ may dwell in your hearts through faith. And I pray that you, being rooted and established in love, may have power, together with all the Lord's holy people, to grasp how wide and long and high and deep is the love of Christ, and to know this love that surpasses knowledge—that you may be filled to the measure of all the fullness of God."
Ephesians 3:17-19 NIV

When we embrace the love of God, we begin to walk in the fruit of God's love as we become more like Him. Every assurance we need in this life's journey is displayed in the love of God. So, rely totally on the love of God that it transmits into knowing the power you have received to subdue the enemy. God loves us so much and has given us the authority to trample upon serpents and scorpions and none shall by any means hurt us. We have been given dominion over this world and we are set to conquer all. It's important to focus more on the love of God over your life than the troubles of the enemy. Continue to fix your gaze on Him and His goodness. My mentor will always say look at your receipts. There is a lot of proof of what God has done for you, sometimes you just need that reminder, and what can stand as a reminder is the goodness of God in your life. Sometimes not just in your life but in the lives of those around you.

Today, I encourage you to walk in the unending love of Christ. Reflect on how God communicated His love to us through Jesus. When I realized that God loves us and looks after us as an individual, it just shows how He is so intentional about us. He does not divide the love He has for us. He does not pour his love into you, then your family member, then another person. That's not how He works. Every second, He keeps showering His love on us. There are billions of people on earth, yet our Heavenly Father watches over us individually, day after day, minute after minute, and second after second. If His eyes are on the sparrow, then rest assured that His eyes are on you every moment. Remember that Christ left the 99 to chase after the one, which is you; It shows how special you are. So, you don't have to fear what the future holds.

Seasons change, happy days come, and bad days come. Our feelings change sometimes depending on the circumstances, but God's love is forever. Humans may love you just for a season, but God loves you regardless of the season. Some people who claim to love you may leave you when it gets difficult, but God will still be right there by your side, ready to walk with you through life. The way you feel in a moment doesn't affect the love God has for you. So, whether you feel fearful, insecure, or unloved, always have that constant reminder that God loves you regardless. Nothing, absolutely nothing, can take away the love of God in your life. Fear can try indefinitely, but what remains a fact is that God loves you unconditionally.

CHAPTER NINE:
MAKE ROOM
FOR THE NEW

"It is truly not a risk, but a certainty that if God wants you to leave the old, then the new is better."

New things cannot effectively grow in an old place. I would like you to think about your closet for a moment. Analyze the size and how occupied it is. What do you do to accommodate new clothes if you have a full closet? You take out some of the old clothes to accommodate the new clothes, right? This is exactly why we can't have the new things God has for us- because we refuse to allow Him to take away the old. God wants you to make room for the new thing(s) He's about to do. One thing I love about our Father is that He has given us the power to choose. Regardless of all the mighty plans and the things God has in store for us, we must first submit and be ready to receive by creating room for things to come into manifestation. Fear is one thing that keeps us in our comfort zone, sometimes accepting something new can be difficult, especially when you have gotten used to what you have.

There was a season in my life when I was content with the things that were happening, and I struggled with making room for what God was going to do in my life. God told me to do certain things in my ladies' ministry that were not the normal for us. I was so afraid of the outcome that it took a while to accept the new way. I had so many thoughts about whether or not people would show up as they did before. I gave excuses for not being equipped and God told me "You are more than equipped for the new."

We can always trust that if it is from God, then it is better than the former. Sometimes, even when new things are exciting, it can come with overwhelming thoughts, and that is understandable. It is something you haven't experienced before, you're not sure what to expect. It could also be that you are not sure if you deserve it or not. Oftentimes, we create boundaries as to what we think we should or should not have, maybe because where we came from does not look like we should have a bright future. I have realized that fear is an underlying cause of not wanting to step into the "new". God has so much in store for us, but fear can be a hinderance to us. If God has told you to do something new, all you have to do is trust him. Let go of the lies the enemy brings. The enemy is fighting because he knows that what is ahead is beneficial to you and detrimental to his kingdom. It is truly not a risk, but a certainty that if God wants you to leave the old, then the new is better. I promise you that one of the best decisions you can make is trusting God in the process of transitioning from the old to the new.

Life in general has different stages and each step takes you to something new. No matter how young you want to remain, each day counts towards you get older. Adulthood is one big change that made me overthink, as I always wished to go back to that dependent little girl. Transitioning to adulthood was a great change for me because I had to level up and become more responsible for myself, my growth, my family, and my ministry. When it comes to life, we sometimes can't do anything about the changes other than be prepared for them. I'm the last child of my parents and still, the baby girl in me would love to be pampered, but I am now in a place where I have embraced my growth. Change is constant, and when it has to do with the change God brings, it can be a hard transition regardless of the blessing. The enemy's plan is to keep you stagnant so that you are too comfortable with the present but I'm here to tell you that there is more. There is more than the present and you need to fully let go to step into it. It's time to let go of whatever is holding you back, and step into the "new". It could be your past, as our past can be a hindrance to us from stepping into the "new". You have to stop holding on to the former things.

"Forget the former things; do not dwell on the past. See, I am doing a new thing! Now it springs up; do you not perceive it?

I am making a way in the wilderness and streams in the wasteland."
Isaiah 43:18-19 NIV

This was the scripture for the year 2023 in my ladies' ministry. Even when God gave me the theme of the year "I WILL DO A NEW THING", I didn't realize that God was about to take us on a journey of letting go of the old. It was a year to let go of a lot of things, people included, particularly for me. God's promises of the "new" require that we release the former things. We need to be repositioned to step into the "new" that God is doing. Don't let fear, guilt, or even laziness hold you captive.

Your past does not determine how God decides to work in your life. God is the one that writes our story so if God wants elevation in chapter five of your life's story, what happened in chapter one is not a criterion for your elevation. It's time to let go of the thoughts of not being good enough. You have hung on to those for too long. It's time to move forward. Looking back is only acceptable when we look to see how far we've come and how far God has brought us. Change is here, and not even your past should hinder it. The "new" is available and not even your background, insecurities, status, or what's in your bank account should stop it. We have a father who does not care where you're coming from. He is a God who meets us right where we are and takes us to where He wants us to be.

What is holding you back today? It might be comfortable but just because it is comfortable doesn't mean it is right for you. You don't want to remain in a place when there is somewhere better. Growth is not how good you are in a thing and remaining stagnant, growth is how you constantly become better. Sometimes we remain stagnant because we refuse to give God a space to have his way.

"Now to him who is able to do immeasurably more than all we ask or

imagine, according to his power that is at work within us."
Ephesians 3:20 NIV

I know the transitioning season can be hard, but you have to believe that what God has for you is better than what you have now. What God has planned for us is beyond our imagination; Starting something new can be difficult, but I can assure you, that if you move when God tells you to move, it never goes wrong.

If God is telling you to move to a new state and you're wondering how to start all over, I'm here to tell you to obey. It could be that you are already settled with your flourishing business, you have friends and family all around and you're just concerned with how the new season will be. If it is God, do not hesitate. If God is telling you to start that business and you're wondering whether or not you will make sales, start and trust God. If God has told you to do something or move somewhere, then it isn't a probability that it will work for your good. God never leaves us stranded.

Take a moment to think about the story of Abraham in the Bible. He couldn't figure out anything when God told him to leave his father's house and go to a place he would show him. Abraham had such a crazy faith to obey, regardless of the fact that he never knew where he was going. Some of you have to change your perspective to "If it is God". There needs to be a shift in our thinking that we get such a crazy faith like Abraham and say, "If it is God, then I trust that it is the best". God only told Abraham how He would be blessed and how he would be great, but everything was determined by Abraham's obedience. When God gives you His promises, you need to be obedient enough to move when He says move, even when it doesn't make sense. We have to move when God says move regardless of how the present circumstances look. Do you know the God we serve? He is a promise keeper. The comfortable place you think you are in at the moment, is one of the least places God wants you to be. The good thoughts you have about God's promises are not even up to a snippet of what God is about to do if you obey.

"But as it is written: "Eye has not seen, nor ear heard, Nor have entered into the heart of man The things which God has prepared for those who love Him."
I Corinthians 2:9 NKJV

This scripture tells us that the eye has not seen, the ear has not heard and it hasn't even come to the thought of man what He has prepared for those who love him. Love is built from a place of trust. So, when you love and trust God, what He has in store for you is something this world can't imagine. You have to trust and believe when God decides to take something away from you in order for Him to birth something new. This just relates to pruning. Pruning is painful but it is needed for the "better" to flourish. A gardener removes certain parts of the trees that are no longer beneficial to the tree. When I say pruning is painful, it is because I have experienced it. As far as I can remember, I've been going through pruning since 2021. I feel like God literally takes us through that season to avoid unnecessary things from getting into our beautiful future. A wise farmer does not depend on the last harvest that he fails to uproot and replant. There must be an uprooting process for the replanting to begin.

"You will still be eating last year's harvest when you will have to move it out to make room for the new."
Leviticus 26:10 NIV

God is the gardener of our lives, and He prunes for our betterment. Pruning bears fruits and all you have to do is to lean on God. When God decides to take you through a pruning season, it doesn't mean you are not doing well, but it does mean that there are even better things inside of you that the world needs to be blessed with.

"He cuts off every branch in me that bears no fruit, while every branch that does bear fruit, he prunes so that it will be even more fruitful."
John 15:2 NIV

I want you to focus on who is working in your life. Focus on God because He is a God that does not fail. What He says surely comes to pass. Trust in His promises and stand on His word because He knows what is best for you. The "new" is available, make room for it!

10 CHAPTER TEN: IT IS ALL FOR A REASON

"I've come to realize that God is not just interested in what He wants to bring out of us but who He wants us to become in the process."

I know you probably have heard this a million times and I'm here to tell you again that everything you're going through or have been through is for a reason. The truth is that God does not waste our pain; He turns it to purpose. I laugh at how the enemy tries to afflict the children of God without the knowledge of how our God does an exchange with the pain. If only the enemy knew how every one of his evil plans are turned to work together for our good, just maybe he would stop trying. But that's his job-to kill, steal, and destroy.

We go through a lot, and we may not have it all figured out, but it's important to note that nothing happens to God's people without a reason. Some of you are in a challenging season, it may look like you're all alone and can't even come out of it. Seasons like this require that we keep our faith and trust that what God wants to birth out of our pain is greater.

"And let us not be weary in doing well; for in due season, we shall reap if we faint not."
Galatians 6:9

In trial seasons, God grows us into who He wants us to be. It is just so beautiful how God turns our tests into testimonies and trials to triumph. When I was going through a fearful season, I reached out to people and the response I got the most was "It is for a reason." It didn't make sense to me until now. I probably wouldn't have written this book if I hadn't experienced the trials. The season doesn't make sense until you start living in the "reason." I think that one thing that may keep someone hopeless, is not knowing the reason ahead of time. It is so important that we keep our hope alive and be sure that what we do expect to come is for our good, and it will be great.

God loves us too much to not give us what we want or take

us to where we want to be, but He wants us to be equipped for all the good things coming. When God allows you to go through certain seasons, it can be that He wants you to feel the same way as the people who will get freed by your experience. Sometimes, even when I know that what I'm going through is for a reason, I still ask God why I needed to go through the season when He can just make the 'reason' come without the season. I've come to realize that God is not just interested in what He wants to bring out of us but who He wants us to become in the process. He is so interested in us becoming more like the nature of Christ. Now, this is love. God can just decide to get whatever He wants from us, but He cares more about the transformation that the season/process brings. If there was one thing the process of being delivered from fear did for me, it humbled me. The same year I was dealing with fear, I became homeless while in school. I had to move out of an apartment I shared with my ex-roommate, even though I still had eight months before my rent was due. It was a tough decision to move out, but I had to do so for my own safety and sanity. It was a lot of stress going to school from my family's house, which was a two-hour drive, while also looking for an apartment. This season was so tough mentally and emotionally that I couldn't fully concentrate in school, and I feared having bad grades. If there was one thing I learned from that situation, it was to be humble enough to know that sometimes homeless people are not lazy people. Life can happen to anyone and sometimes we may not know what people go through until we walk in their shoes. 2021 is one of the years that I look back on and exclaim God's goodness because even when I prayed, it didn't look like I would get out of that season, but God brought me out of it even stronger. Looking back at my journey, I can say that sometimes it can be hard to realize how much God is blessing us because it didn't happen all at once.

"I consider that our present sufferings are not worth comparing

with the glory that will be revealed in us."
Romans 8:18 NIV

I want you to look through your journals in the past years. There are things God has brought you out of even when you never thought you would come out. Now, this should tell you that what you're going through at this moment is going to birth a glory tomorrow that will be unrecognizable. If we can have this Faith then we won't be disturbed, because if God did it before, He can do it again. There are people that are about to be freed through your story. Your situation is not just about you, there are people tied to the purpose God is bringing out of the pain. There are destinies tied to your purpose.

When people reach out to me to pray for their healing, I get even more compassionate because I've walked in that pain. It is easy to free people when you've walked in that part and have experienced freedom yourself. It is at this moment that we extend what we have received. You have been freed to walk others to freedom. So, the next time you get into a tough situation, focus on what God is about to birth from it. The pain can make it seem like God is far away, but He is right there with you and in the process, God is preparing you for the blessing.

You have to continuously speak positively in this season and say, 'though I may not know when the pain will be over, I choose to trust God to bring me out on His own timing.' God does not just look at our present, He is concerned with our future. The plans He has for us are more than we can ever imagine.

When you're in pain, you should run to your Father- God. Pain can make us realize how much we need God. The season of fear I went through made me run to God because that is where deliverance lies. My relationship with God today has grown as a result of my state of brokenness. It was in that season that I completely surrendered all to God. One prayer I always prayed before 2021 was that God allows me to go through whatever painful sessions so long as He will bring me out of it. It's a good prayer but, at that time, I was so focused on the glory that I didn't really realize how painful the process was. I would listen to people's stories and how God brought them far. I was so impressed by their present blessings that I thought that the pain they experienced to get there wasn't so bad. When you see people who are now walking in the purpose of their pain and enjoying the blessing, don't get so enticed that you forget that they had to go through an uncomfortable process to arrive there.

I had to rephrase my prayer to 'Lord, please equip me for every season that will come in order for me to birth the reason/purpose.' God is so intentional about us and nothing happens without His awareness. Everything God has in store for us is worth our patience. If you're in a season of your life that seems discouraging, I would love you to listen to the song "Seasons" by Benjamin William Hastings and Hillsong Worship. When I was going through a fearful season of my life, this was one of the songs I played. Almost every night I went into my bathroom and cried to God while this song was on repeat. I wasn't sure what God was doing behind the scenes, but I kept hope alive. I cried to God several times to make all the trials I faced pass me, but it had to happen according to His timing. We always have those moments when we want God to take the pain away from us especially when the timing looks so long from our perspective. As much as we trust God for what He wants to birth out of our pain, it's important that we also trust when He will birth the glory. His timing is perfect and way different from our timing.

I can't talk about that season of my life without pointing out how grateful I am for those that stood by me in that season. One thing I don't want you to ever do is to isolate yourself from the people God has sent to help you in certain seasons. God is our ultimate helper, but the truth is that He uses man (humans). There are people God has placed in your life that can help by encouraging you and enabling you to see the light in your pain. We are truly not meant to do this life alone. Through God's direction, get yourself a community of believers who will pour into you and pick you up when you fall. It's okay to fall but it's terrible to not have anyone to lift you back up. If you're going through any tough season right now, I want you to know that it is temporary. Be okay with the moment knowing that God has placed you there for a reason, which is greater than the present. Stay faithful in the moment because something bigger is coming. Live in the moment and make it profitable because it is preparation for what is to come. One day, you will look back to where God brought you from and you will realize that the pain wasn't wasted. You will realize that God really had your best interest at heart. In the moment, continue to allow God to shape you for the future. This too will pass!

It is just a season for a reason.

11

CHAPTER ELEVEN: DIVINELY SEPARATED FOR A PURPOSE

"Do not allow people to stymie what God wants to do in and through you. Do not let the fear of losing people make you hold onto who you should be separated from."

Separation unto God is one aspect of a believer's life that we cannot run from if we truly want to be where God wants us to be. A lot of times, we tend to expect everyone around us to walk this same life. Some adjustments can't be made in our lives if we're surrounded by certain people, or if we are trying to engage everyone in our life's journey. Some people can be a hindrance to your process of becoming who God wants you to be. I know it's exciting to have everyone you love and are familiar with become a partner in your journey, but God wants us to solely focus on Him and what He's called us to do without being cluttered by everyone. If we truly want to walk in fulfillment, anyone who should walk this life with us must be based on God's direction. The story of Abraham explains how things didn't go as planned because Abraham carried his family along with him when God told him, and only him, to move at the moment. First, Lot's wife was disobedient and looked back, which made her become a pillar of salt. Another moment when Abraham realized there needed to be a separation between him and Lot, was when they had so many possessions that the present land couldn't accommodate. You need to know that everything God does is in our best interest. It may not look like it at the moment, but I can assure you that it is the best.

When I talk about the year 2021, you will see how I walked in uncomfortable situations. Outside of everything I went through that year, I still had to go through a season of separation. God decided to allow a lot to happen at once in my life, regardless of the discomfort. Going through a season of separation, at a time when I thought I needed many people around me to walk me through my tough season and sympathize with me, was very hard. Alot of people left me and I also had to leave some friends. One thing about God is He cares more about the best for you than He cares about you being comfortable. There is a lot that God wants to do in your life that requires you to be separated unto Him. When I talk about separation, I don't mean isolation. Isolation gives the devil access to do his work in your life. It is very important to have people in your life who listen to God and submit to Him.

Even in my season of separation, I still had very few prominent people in my life who God assigned to walk me through the journey. The good thing about these people was that they viewed everything from God's perspective. They told me the truth even when I didn't want to hear it. Now, those are the kind of people God wants you to walk through life with and not people who will be so familiar with you that they pity you out of God's glory. When I talk about separation, God doesn't separate you from who is for you, instead, He separates you from who isn't for you. It is so beautiful having real people in your life and that is what God wants for you. I really do not fancy having a lot of people in my life if they do not have my best interest at heart. I would prefer to have a few people who are for me.

It's important to know that when God gave you the vision, He didn't give it to everyone else, so you cannot expect to take other people on a ride they weren't given tickets to. People can become a distraction when they do not understand the vision. They can tell you what they think is the right thing to do but you must remember who you heard - God. This is why we must be careful in choosing friends and generally who we accept into our lives. Friendship is so big for me so I'm not ready to settle with someone who God hasn't assigned to be my friend. When you know the calling upon your life, you start praying about the people that come into your life, so you know where to place them. You can't give people permanent positions in your life when they are just meant to be for a season. The people we have in our life play a major role in either making or destroying us. They can either stop us from fulfilling our purpose or push us to be purposeful.

So, when God is pruning people out of the garden of your life, be calm because you don't know what they would have destroyed, and you don't know what God has seen that you can't see. Do not allow people to stymie what God wants to do in and through you. Do not let the fear of losing people make you hold onto who you should be separated from. I know the fear that comes with having to separate from people you love irrespective of their toxicity. A lot of people want to just settle for less because they are afraid of being left alone. It is better to be alone for a period of time and trust God to give you the best, than to be with people or someone that disrupts your peace and growth. It could be a toxic relationship or friendship you're not willing to let go, or it's an environment you aren't willing to leave. All you need to do is to trust God and know that if He wants you to be separated from the people or the environment, then it is all for your good.

I don't want to focus so much on people that I forget to mention that we must be separated from sin to fully attain the heights God wants us to attain. Anything that separates you from God is something you should separate yourself from. God should be our first priority. I can understand the world we live in, and it can sometimes be a struggle to walk in the path of righteousness when others around you are doing otherwise. But remember that we are in this world but not of this world. As hard as it can be, it is possible to live a holy life through the help of the Holy Spirit. One thing God strongly dislikes is sin but even if we fall, we are so blessed to have a God who forgives. Whenever you fall into sin, a separation happens, but you can run to God for reconciliation. When we sin, the enemy puts guilt and shame on us so that we run away from our creator. If we can see things differently, we will know that it is in that moment we fall short that we are expected to go even more closer to God.

"But your iniquities have separated you from your God; your sins have hidden his face from you, so that he will not hear."
Isaiah 59:2 NIV

Every minute, the devil fights to make us separated from God but we have to fight back, be separated from sin and embrace righteousness. We live in a messy world where righteousness and holiness are not held in high regard, but we can always stand for the truth as believers and refuse to fear what others will think of or say about us. You were not created to fit into the world's standards, you were created to be different. God has chosen you to be different in this world full of chaos, so do not dim your light. The Bible says "For you were once darkness, but now you are light in the Lord. Live as children of light" in Ephesians 5:8 NIV.

I'm challenging you today to allow God to separate you for His glory. Will it be painful? Yes. In 2022, I experienced separation from a friendship I thought was long-term. I cried and wished this friend could walk this journey with me, but God sees and knows better, and He said no. That friendship was one I could boldly say I invested my time in, but it didn't go the way I though it would. In that moment, I closed the walls of my heart and was not ready to open up. I used the scripture "Guard your heart with all diligence" as an excuse to make my relationship with others unfruitful. This scripture was never meant for you to block your heart rather, it says guard your heart. Have you ever visited a palace with guards mounted by the gate? Do they automatically create a restriction that no one can enter? No. Instead, people who come to visit are properly assessed before going in. This is what it means to guard your heart. If we continue to close the gate of our hearts towards people, we will also miss those who are for us.

When we find ourselves in situations that require us to separate from a certain person, we need to accept what God allows and be thankful for the moments we have spent with that person. Truly, not everyone is meant to be in our life for a lifetime. Be thankful for the reason and the season, and be assured that God will keep connecting you to good people. It's definitely not an easy decision to separate yourself from people you love dearly, but sometimes God wants you to love from a distance. If they are close, they can contaminate the assignment God has given to you. If God is calling you to a place of separation, I want you to go without hesitation. Do not let your disobedience or fear of losing people hinder you from what God has in store for you. Also, if there is an area in your life or a habit that is holding you hostage, it's time to separate from it. God wants you to separate from everything that keeps you from Him. He wants your all today. Give it to Him.

12

CHAPTER TWELVE: CONFIDENT IN CHRIST

"In fact, confidence in Christ is when you are insecure in yourself but decide to step into the confidence God gives."

Growing up in church, joining the choir at age six and being the little girl that loved to be seen and heard, I had a very high level of confidence, especially when it had to do with Godly activities. I took my first ever leadership role in the choir at age nine as the financial secretary. Then, I loved the role of a lead singer, not caring about how people viewed me or whether or not I could sing to their satisfaction. Of course, I was singing to God even though I didn't have a full knowledge of what I was doing at that time. Children's day was every second week of August, and we couldn't wait for that day. It really felt like the choristers were special people different from the audience. We did all we could to be on our best behavior when it approached children's day because no one wanted to ever go on suspension. I mean, this day is a day we all get to perform before our parents and visitors in the church's main auditorium. We were trained to be so disciplined as little choristers as the church always had an eye on the choir seats which were just beside the altar. I got into a fight one time during the week of the children's day celebration which means I had only just a little percentage of hope to sing on the main day. If tears could rush down like rainfall, my tears could have filled plenty bottles. As one of the leaders of the choir, there was a double punishment if you were involved in a fight. I had already been given a song as a lead solo and at that point I just knew it couldn't be me any longer. I did all I could, wrote an apology letter and asked some friends to plead on our behalf. Somehow, we were forgiven and given the opportunity to sing on the children's day. This was who I was as a child. I was never shy and I always wanted to be seen.

Thinking about who I turned out to be years later, I would have rejoiced in that situation knowing that I no longer have the role and wouldn't be seen by an audience.

Something happened to me when I was 10 years old. I got

into a boarding school in my JSS1 (grade 7), and it changed everything. Normally, in Nigeria, you are obliged to call those in higher grades with a title attached to their names-Senior. This means if I'm in grade 7, I should call a student in grade 8 and higher, with a title before their names, e.g Senior Rejoice. That didn't make sense to me because what's the point? Aside from that, I got bullied by these seniors and slowly began to have low self-esteem. You wouldn't believe the "confident Rejoice" stopped talking and decided to go mute about every situation. Seniors would take your stuff and use it without your consent, your items get stolen, and people talk down on you pointing out what they had that you didn't have. This was so new to me and I was gradually getting into a terrible psychological state. I lost all the confidence I had built in Christ. Even though I didn't know what it meant to be confident in Christ, I can tell now what it is. Somehow, even when I tried to get back up, everything happening seemed to be a culture I had to just get adjusted to. The culture was that junior students go through some sort of bullying, become seniors, and retaliate against the upcoming juniors. I said to myself "just get along with the culture and the juniors better get ready to go through just what I went through in the hands of the present seniors." I didn't realize how this changed me to have a "pay back" mindset instead of finding healing and extending it to others coming after me. Boarding school was never a place I wanted to be but at that time it was believed that it helps students become more disciplined. I was fortunate to have my sister who was a class ahead of me in the same boarding school as she became a shoulder to cry on. All I wanted to do was go home because I couldn't deal with the bullying and all the abuse I was going through.

I found myself indulging in entertainment to boost my confidence. I wrote songs that resonated with the problems of the school just as a form of ridicule and the students loved it. During night classes when I should be reading, I was taken by seniors to different classes to sing and entertain others. I was showered with love by seniors just because of what I did to make them feel good. I was gradually losing my identity to the world. My school had a choir which I never belonged to. I had a voice to sing for the glory of God yet, all I did was sing worldly songs for the vain glorification of people. My academic performance in JSS1(grade 7) was nothing you want to hear about.

I knew I had lost my true identity in finding an identity to fit in this world. I knew I had a greater calling and that there was more for me in Christ. I left boarding school after grade 7 because in as much as I outwardly felt good about the appraisal of people, I knew I was slowly losing who I was with all of the bullying and abuse. My parents had heard my complaints about not wanting to be in a boarding school any longer, so they gave me a chance to choose a day school instead. After I left, I had to start dealing with the traumatic experiences from boarding school. I noticed I became very shy, silencing my voice even when I needed to speak. I struggled with low self-esteem for years and it was so evident. I struggled with speaking to people about how I felt or giving my opinion. I knew I had a voice, and I needed to use it. When God started telling me about being a speaker, as much as I knew that was what I should be doing, it felt weird. So many thoughts of what feedback I would get from those listening made me limit myself. Because I used to be a people pleaser, it made me think of how people would see me if I started speaking. Somehow, inside of me, I still had that boldness, and I knew there was something in me to bless the world. Regardless of being timid, I still decided to be optimistic and start somewhere.

I spoke to myself about my future in the mirror. Before I began receiving invitations to speak, I acted as a speaker in front of my siblings. I am a dreamer, and I knew my voice wouldn't just be heard locally but globally. These were some lines I acted in front of my siblings:

Me as the moderator: All the way from Nigeria, let's welcome our next speaker, Rejoice.

Me as the audience: claps and shouts...

Me as the speaker (Rejoice): Thank you so much for having me. It's such an honor to be here. Greetings from my home country Nigeria. I was given the topic...

I seriously don't know how my siblings accommodated my drama because this seems so crazy. As young as 12, I started writing an autobiography of my future on paper. I always wrote "My name is Rejoice Oluomachi Anusi and I'm from Uturu in Abia State, Nigeria. I am a Woman and Child Rights Activist whose vision is to see that women enjoy equal rights and children are properly educated and taken care of." Of course, maybe the English wasn't well constructed then, but I dreamt big. As much as I know I'm not officially a Woman and Child's Rights Activist, now that my ministry is focused on women and children, I believe that God was giving me a desire for my future calling.

Recently, I found a rough book where I wrote an article when I was 15 years old on the topic "Wisdom." I went ahead to write "All rights reserved. No part of this book should be copied or reprinted...". What's funny to me is that, I actually pirated and was informing others not to pirate. I didn't really understand what it meant though. All I'm trying to point out is that 'I DARED TO DREAM!' Regardless of my fears, I pushed through. If I did it, you can do it. Everything I did sounds funny but I didn't know that God was (in His own way), preparing me for the future. It looks crazy but we serve a God that uses the things that look like it has no sense to bring up interesting things.

"and the base things of the world and the things which are despised God has chosen, and the things which are not, to bring to nothing the things that are,"
I Corinthians 1:28 NKJV

In June 2020, after seeing a movie titled "Alter Ego" I knew it was time to speak and be a voice to those who couldn't speak up. The movie described how ladies were sexually and physically abused because they were at the mercies of a particular man. This man provided shelter for the homeless girls, gave them a good education and health care but went behind to subject them to physical and sexual molestation. The ladies had to suffer, until a woman who was a lawyer stood up to fight for them. I was immediately motivated to start my ministry. I wasn't sure what I was doing that afternoon after seeing this movie. I told my sister I was creating a WhatsApp group for ladies. I got the name "Fabulous Ladies Foundation," and I asked God what the vision was because I couldn't start without having a sneak peek of what we wanted to achieve. I had a pen and a book, and God said the vision is to "raise fulfilled ladies". Everything that happened that day was truly not planned but I had a push to start immediately. I started with no idea of what having a ministry looked like. I didn't even know it was an actual ministry at the time.

As I mentioned earlier, I wanted to become an advocate for women and children when I grew up. I didn't study law, but I knew it wasn't required to be a voice for those who couldn't speak for themselves. When I started ministry, God told me that there's more to it than just speaking up for ladies. He said He will use me as a vessel to give the ladies a voice to speak up for themselves and others around them. That was the journey of me becoming a speaker and it was definitely not an easy one. Gradually, I began to understand who I am in Christ and what I have been called to do. It wasn't a smooth journey and to be honest, I am still on the journey of knowing who I am in Christ. Because we are not called to fit into this world, but called to stand out, daring to be different can be difficult. But it is worth it and God will bring people your way who are on the same path as you are and standing in line with who God says you are regardless of what others do or say to you.

Standing for Christ in high school was one of the hardest decisions I had to make. I was called names, even by assumed believers, and was said I do the 'Jesus thing' too much. Many people told me that I was only being good because I still lived with my parents and that I would change when I got to college. Did I fear falling off faith? Yes. In fact, when I got into college I was trying to fit into the world until covid hit and I stepped into my purpose. Covid was a blessing to me as it was a calm moment that made me think. Outside of schooling, working, and just other day to day activities, what can I really be doing that is not based on an earthly reward? What can I do and feel joyful without being paid for it? I know a lot of people who birthed their ministries, businesses and stepped authentically into their calling during Covid.

The experiences I had that affected my confidence were just a few of what the kids and teenagers in this generation experience. Our kids and teenagers are going through so much more than we know, and they need help more than ever before. We live in a generation that portrays everything to be perfect on the internet which makes kids and young adults begin to compare themselves and feel unworthy. We have a real job to do with the kids and young adults of this generation. The thought of making quick money just to fit in is destroying this young generation. The fear of not feeling like they belong has made so many of them lose their identity to the world. Our youth could benefit from God-confidence, which springs up from knowing who they are in Christ and not a type of self-confidence from the world's view of who they are. If we continue to chase the things the world gives just to have a sense of being, then it is like chasing the wind. There is a void that only God can fill. The things of the world, the success of the world and everything it gives cannot give you the joy and peace that you need. Can it make you happy? Yes. Happiness is an outward look but when we talk about joy, it happens internally and transforms you externally. God is so intentional about you that He didn't bring you into this world without a drafted plan. There is a path He has placed us on and the only way we can fulfill our purpose here on earth is by working that path. We lose track when we begin to compare ourselves with others and their achievements. I believe we will live better and be full of joy if we are committed to our lane. I have noticed that comparison is a major hindrance to our fulfillment on earth. I'm not just talking about the kids and young adults, but also about the grown adults. It's so easy to compare ourselves to others and not focus on our own path. We all have a role to play and just like the body of Christ, we are meant to complement each other. No one, I repeat, no one can effectively work on your path for you, and you can never get to your destination through someone else's path. We all have different journeys for the fulfillment of the kingdom of God here on earth. If we are busy trying to be someone else, who will be the person God had called us to be? Who will be able to do that which only you have been equipped to do? Who will show up for the people you have been assigned to show up for?

I wish we can view life beyond who does 'better' and focus on 'who is authentically walking on the path God wants them to walk on.' Just as the eyes can't function as the legs, so it is to our assignment. We are unique beings!

When it comes to being confident, I am still on my journey of healing from the trauma that caused my low self-esteem in the past. I can look back and be grateful for how far I've come. A lady reached out to me some time ago asking how she could speak confidently in a speech that she was about to give. In my head I was like 'oh, I think you reached out to the wrong person.' She was a colleague in school and a follower of my YouTube channel. I assumed she reached out because she viewed one of my videos. I explained how sometimes we have to overlook our insecurities and do what we have to do because it's bigger than us. One thing I do before speaking is try to avoid glorifying 'how' I speak more than 'what' I speak. We have to come to a point where we do what we have to do, even when we are shy or afraid of people's feedback. When speaking to people, forget about what they may say about how you speak. Be rest assured that there are some people, or maybe just one person, who will be blessed. I don't speak because I am confident, but I decide to accept the task that God wants me to complete, even in my weakness, because it is in my weakness His strength is made perfect. Think about it this way, if you were confident and had it all together, you probably wouldn't need the boldness God gives. Sometimes God allows us to feel how we feel so that we can understand that we can do nothing on our own. I'm challenging you today to do it even when you're afraid. Do it even when you're nervous. The problem is not your insecurities, the problem comes when you're hindered by those insecurities. In fact, confidence in Christ is when you are insecure in yourself but decide to step into the confidence God gives. It is when you look pass the hindrances and decide to do what God has called you to do regardless.

It's time to stop idolizing your insecurities. You have all the confidence that you need in Christ!

13

CHAPTER THIRTEEN: DEAL WITH IT

"When you run away from something that you should face head on, you end up repeating the same cycle."

There is only one way to overcome fear, and it is to deal with it. When you pray, you're dealing with fear. When you dig deep into God's word, you are dealing with fear. When you control your thoughts, you are dealing with fear. When you lean into God's love, you are dealing with fear. Running away from your fear is just like postponing your battles. I once heard that any process you run away from also comes back haunting you. Why run away from something you can deal with or will still have to deal with?

When you run away from something that you should face head on, you end up repeating the same cycle. Sometimes we complain of how things keep repeating themselves in our lives. The truth is you have probably refused to get to the root and uproot it completely. Cutting off the leaves and branches does not remove the root of a tree. When we don't deal with something today, we allow it to come back even stronger.

In my experience of struggling with fear, I looked for ways to run away from it. I used to wish a friend could just come visit and sleep over so I wouldn't have to sleep alone. What I didn't know was that someone being with me for the moment only stopped the fear for the moment, but it wasn't dealt with. I prayed that I would wake up with all my feelings of fear gone, but nothing changed until I made up my mind to fight with the strength God had given to me. I had to deal with the fear of my future by stepping into who God has called me to be. Did I feel fearful starting ministry? Yes. But I had to deal with that fear by doing it afraid. Everything I set out to do, at some point, I felt fearful about, but I did it regardless. We have the advantage of not having to deal with our fears alone. We have a God walking us through every step of our journey.

One thing about God is that He is not just interested in

removing the circumstance, but He is also interested in changing you through that circumstance. If God removed fear from my life without the process of dealing with it, there is a lot that I wouldn't have accomplished. One of which is this book you are reading. I never thought I could write a book until God gave me this story to tell after my journey of overcoming fear. I had a desire to write a book, but never thought I would write well.

Whenever I go through something, I love to ask God the reason He is making me go through it. Even when the situation is bad, the truth is that God will never let you go through something without birthing the glory. I got to know the power of the Word of God when I decided to deal with fear. Dealing with fear was a tough process but I knew for sure that I would one day look back and be joyful that God allowed the situation, not just for my benefit, but for the benefit of those assigned to me. I want you to focus on what God is birthing out of your situation more than focusing on the situation. Approaching it this way will help us intentionally deal with the situation and see the glory.

I'm so grateful for how God used my parents to hold me accountable in fighting the battle of fear. I didn't realize what my dad did for me by stopping my mom from sleeping with me in the same room. My parents understood the battle and decided to cover me in prayers but yet, allowed me to handle the sword. These were my dad's words "When you allow the spirit of fear to dominate you, you just tell God how much you don't believe in Him and His power over fear. When you let fear have its power over you, you are making room for the devil to do more evil". As much as I thought my parents weren't being considerate about my situation and how I was spiritually attacked, now I can look back and be thankful for their decision. I cried and severally asked God if I wasn't too young to be going through what I went through. I had to fight and claim the victory that has already been won by Christ.

The story of David and Goliath is one story that I will always love to talk about whenever I think of overcoming fear. You can take your time to study 1 Samuel chapter 17 in the Bible. The battle between the Philistines and the Israelites was a battle that would have been humanly concluded to be won by the Philistines because of how they looked outwardly. They appeared physically fit for the battle and they had a giant, Goliath, who has been a wart from his youth. With the look of things, it was a certainty that he should win the battle. The Israelites already saw themselves in the hands of the Philistines but there came David, who dared to face his fears and deal with it. It wasn't just his fears but all the Israelites, yet he decided to win the battle regardless. When we face our fears, we do not only win a personal battle, but we win a battle for the people who have been assigned to us. Our victory leads others to their victory.

David was given apparel to look fit for the battle, but he took it off because he understood the assignment. The Israelites did not realize that it wasn't about the physical looks, it was spiritual clothing which is the armor of Christ. The battle you fight requires you to put on the full armor of Christ. Goliath laughed at David and could already see how he would ruin David's life, but he never knew that David came with a spiritual strategy. David picked up just five stones to fight against someone who was physically covered. He didn't care what the giant looked like, as he was more concerned about who was inside of him, God. He knew that the person in him is greater than anything in the world. He understood that he wasn't just fighting a physical battle, but he was fighting a spiritual battle that needed a spirit, which was the spirit of God, inside of him. Just a stone brought the Philistine down. Maybe for you it's just a word from the Bible. Maybe it's just a time of prayer. Maybe it's just a positive thought.

It's time for you to face that fear. It may look big but the God you serve is bigger. You don't have to run from something you have been spiritually equipped to fight. One lesson I gained from the success story of David is that he was spiritually prepared even without an invitation. The enemy keeps moving, seeking for whom to devour. Therefore, you must be equipped for the battle so that when it comes, you will be able to fight against it. You have to always be in your kit which is the armor of Christ.

"Put on the full armor of God, so that you can take your stand against the devil's schemes. For our struggle is not against flesh and blood, but against the rulers, against the authorities, against the powers of this dark world, and against the spiritual forces of evil in the heavenly realms. Therefore put on the full armor of God, so that when the day of evil comes, you may be able to stand your ground, and after you have done everything, to stand. Stand firm then, with the belt of truth buckled around your waist, with the breastplate of righteousness in place, and with your feet fitted with the readiness that comes from the gospel of peace. In addition to all this, take up the shield of faith, with which you can extinguish all the flaming arrows of the evil one. Take the helmet of salvation and the sword of the Spirit, which is the word of God. And pray in the Spirit on all occasions with all kinds of prayers and requests. With this in mind, be alert and always keep on praying for all the Lord's people. Pray also for me, that whenever I speak, words may be given to me so that I will fearlessly make known the mystery of the gospel, for which I am an ambassador in chains. Pray that I may declare it fearlessly, as I should." Ephesians 6:11-20 NIV

This Bible verse sums it up. Don't run away from your fears. You're a child of God and He has already overcome the world of which fear is included. You have all it takes to overcome fear. You have the spirit of God inside of you and He's all that you need. It's time to take your position and defeat fear.

14

CHAPTER FOURTEEN: NO LONGER SLAVES

"Choosing not to worry about tomorrow can be difficult especially when our 'today' doesn't give a sense of hope but it's important to always live in the present and give everything to God remembering who we are to Him-His child."

I want you to take a moment and proclaim these words "I AM NO LONGER A SLAVE TO FEAR, I AM A CHILD OF GOD." These words are so powerful as they reaffirm where you now belong. You belong to the family of the most high King therefore, the power fear had over you has been lost. You have to keep affirming these words, give no room for fear and send it back to where it belongs. You are God's heir, and you should inherit everything from Him. Fear is not of God, so it is not part of your inheritance. You have been born into the family of God from the moment you accepted His son as your lord and savior. God chose you right from your mother's womb even when you didn't choose Him.

"The Spirit you received does not make you slaves, so that you live in fear again; rather, the Spirit you received brought about your adoption to sonship. And by him we cry, "Abba, Father." The Spirit himself testifies with our spirit that we are God's children."
Romans 8:15-16 NIV

College is such a different world and sometimes I can't explain the things I've experienced. You meet people from totally different backgrounds and you're not sure who they truly are. Whenever I get attacked spiritually and I call my mom to let her know, she will always tell me "Remember who you are; you are a child of God, and nothing can harm you". This stands as a reminder to me whenever I'm tempted to fall back to fear because, to be honest, there are times when situations trigger me to be so fearful that I forget where and who I belong to. I always tell people to stand firm on what they believe. If you're a Christian, stand firm on where you belong because you don't know what other people are committed to or whom they belong to.

Have you seen any movie that portrays a King's palace with his slaves? Do you see how the slaves do everything in fear because they're at the mercy of the King? That is exactly how we act when we allow ourselves to be enslaved by fear. We let ourselves be controlled by the devil through fear, forgetting who we belong to, God. You have received the spirit of God and He dwells in you. The Holy Spirit brought us boldness and not fear. The next time fear comes knocking at the door of your life, proclaim where and who you belong to and rebuke it in the name of Jesus.

One night in 2021, after so many spiritual attacks, I had to speak loudly and reproclaim that I belong to Jesus and that the enemy has no power over me. God has given us the spirit of boldness instead of fear. Realizing that you're a child of the one who created the universe changes everything about you. Why will you let fear, insecurities, depression, or guilt dwell in a life where the most high King dwells. Your body is the temple of God and his spirit dwells in you. I'm praying that we find our true identity in Christ so that we may be able to respond to the enemy with who we know we are. When we truly know who we are, we will trust in our Father and rely on him for our life's journey. The beautiful thing is that, as a child of God, you have the Holy Spirit right inside you. He is there to guide you through life's journey.

One of the fears I dealt with was the fear of tomorrow. I believe that I had not realized the help I have been given to rely on God, even in the affairs of my tomorrow. I had thoughts of how my future would turn out, if I would make terrible mistakes that I would live to regret, or if I would be a failure. These thoughts hindered my knowledge of what it means to be a child of God. I feared the uncertainties of the future without realizing that God had it all figured out.

Choosing not to worry about tomorrow can be difficult especially when our 'today' doesn't give a sense of hope but it's important to always live in the present and give everything to God remembering who we are to Him-His child. He created us and has our lives all planned out and what He has in store for us is beyond our imagination. The truth is that God has such a beautiful plan for us, but we sometimes drift away from the path He has placed us on. It's one thing for God to plan and it's another thing for us to walk in accordance with His plan. The Bible says: "And we know that in all things God works for the good of those who love him, who have been called according to his purpose." Romans 8:28 NIV

Let's dwell a little on the phrase "according to his purpose". The dictionary defines purpose as 'the reason for which something is done or created or for which something exists'. We lose sight of who we are when our way of living does not align with our purpose. I believe that one of the reasons why we remain in bondage of the enemy is because we do not know who we are. Finding your purpose starts from accepting Christ. It is in the process of knowing Him that you find your identity in him. The question "Who are you?" is a very prominent question in our daily lives. Let's look at the story of the evil spirit overpowering the seven sons of Sceva.

"One day the evil spirit answered them, "Jesus I know, and Paul I know about, but who are you?"" Acts 19:15 NIV

Even the evil spirits could ask this question because they understood the power of "Identity". When we do not know who we are, the enemy continues to mess with us. The devil knows who we are, who is inside of us and the power we have over him when we know who we are. This is why he strives to put lies into our minds so that we forget who and whose we are. This reminds me of my younger days. When we engage in a fight, one of the most common words we say or hear is "Who do you think you are?" This particular question was never answered by words but by winning the fight. I don't know about others, but when I got that question, I had two options: (1) win the fight over my opponent or (2) accept defeat. It's so funny but this is what should happen when the enemy comes questioning us. It doesn't just end by saying you're a child of God but, it must reflect on who wins the battle. If you've truly found your identity in Christ, then you will be able to give the enemy the right answer by not allowing him to win.

Some Christians struggle with their identity in Christ. We try to fit into the world's narrative by doing what's accepted in the world and unaccepted in the word-God's word. We forget that God never created us to fit into the world's standard but to stand true to where we belong. Knowing who and whose we are changes the way we approach our day-to-day living. The enemy will always come to put negative thoughts in our minds like "I am not good enough, I'm unloved, I'm ugly", but we can decide to listen to what our father- God says we are. God says we are loved and good enough, he says we are wonderfully and fearfully made. God says we are free from guilt, fear, condemnation and we are no more slaves to the enemy, but we are his children. You have to see yourself as God sees you. Also, we cannot proclaim to be children of God if our lifestyle doesn't reflect Christ. People should be able to look at our lives and see Jesus. We are living epistles, which means that our lives are being read and people want to see who you say you are by the way you live your life. We can't claim to be children of God and still act like those under the captivity of the enemy. When we say we are no longer slaves, we mean we are no longer slaves to sin, fear, depression, shame and every other thing that the enemy enslaved you with.

Evangelizing on campus is one of the most beautiful things I enjoy doing whenever I get to do so. Just after our classes one day, I, and some other people in my fellowship, decided to evangelize in school. I was paired with a girl, and we decided to preach at a place called "Love Garden." This is my favorite place to preach because it's a place where you see people sitting just to chill, reflect, wait for someone, hang out with others, etc. I noticed a guy sitting at one corner with his air pods in his ear. My evangelism partner opted that we go share the gospel with him. When we got there, exchanged pleasantries and it was time to pray, my partner asked if his music was still on. It was funny to hear that he wasn't listening to anything; he just put it on for whatever reason. In the cause of preaching to him about the love God has over us and how He sent His only son, Jesus, to die for our sins, I received a question. I love when it gets to the point where it turns to an interaction, but I normally would be praying in my heart that the Holy Spirit helps me to stay balanced when answering the questions because truthfully, people have a lot of questions to ask, especially young people. This was His question "If God truly loves us and has our best interest at heart, why did He give us the right to choose knowing that our will could lead us astray?" To be honest, this was truly a hard question that I had to exhale before responding. Thank God for the Holy Spirit. I asked Him a question in return "If God controlled your will, would you ever feel He loves you?" The truth is that Love is never forced. What difference are we to slaves if we were automatically controlled by someone that says He loves us? God wants us to serve Him from a place of joy and free will. We have been given the will to choose what is right. We have the will to accept God's love by accepting Jesus into our life and allowing Him to take charge. He desires a relationship, and a relationship is not formed by force but by choice.

Accepting Jesus does not make us slaves to Him, but sons

guided by our father-God. Think about a slave. A slave does everything His master says without thinking whether or not it is for his best interest. Of course, almost all the time, it is in his master's best interest. But, think about a loving master, God, who shows you what is good and evil, yet advises you to choose the good for your benefit. At the garden of Eden, Adam and Eve broke the covenant which at the time created a demarcation but God, in His infinite mercy, sent His only son to die and reconcile us back to Him. On that very day, just when Jesus said, 'IT IS FINISHED', the veil was torn. Everything screamed 'YE ARE NO MORE SLAVES BUT SONS.' On that very day, we were let loose from the bondage of the enemy. The chains of slavery were broken, and we received a crown of Sonship.

When Adam and Eve ate the forbidden fruit in the garden of Eden, there was a separation as the communion they had with God was broken. This caused them to be afraid of their creator who they had sweet fellowship with. They feared speaking to God because of the shame that accompanied their sin.

"He answered, "I heard you in the garden, and I was afraid because I was naked; so I hid.""
Genesis 3:10 NIV

Sin causes us to hide but the truth is that when we fall short, the better place to run is to the presence of your father, God. The enemy tried to separate us from God, but Jesus paid the price on the Cross of Calvary which tore the veil and gave us access to the father. What the enemy wants to do is blind you from receiving the freedom that Jesus brought through His death and resurrection. You are God's heir and no more should you be enslaved by the enemy.

"So you are no longer a slave, but God's child; and since

you are his child, God has made you also an heir."
Galatians 4:7 NIV

Say this prayer if you feel bonded by fear, sin, guilt or any insecurities.

"Dear Lord Jesus, thank you for what you did for me on the cross. Thank you for not giving up on me. Thank you for the reconciliation you made for me to the father. I receive the freedom you have given me, and I proclaim that I am no longer a slave to the enemy. I am a child of the most high king." Amen.

If you said this prayer, congratulations on your acceptance to the freedom Christ brought to you. You are loved and you belong to the lineage of Christ. You are a son and no longer a slave!

15

CHAPTER FIFTEEN: TRUST THE PROCESS

"If we get so interested in the finished product that we become absent in the process, we may also remove ourselves from the promise."

The journey to overcoming fear can really be challenging. It is all a process, and we need to strive to make it progressive. It's easy to hear/say "Trust the process", but it can be difficult to apply it especially when life seems overwhelming. Questions like "How do I trust the process when I'm not even okay with the process?" can run through our minds daily. Trusting the process sometimes is not really about "trusting the process", but it's about trusting the one, God, who is allowing you to go through the process. When you trust God, you can trust what He is putting you through. Every journey God lets you embark on, is never a journey to walk through alone. I hear God saying, 'I just want you to hold My hands and let me lead you through.'

The truth is that I still sometimes struggle to this day. There are times where it gets really overwhelming, and I ask God why the process is even necessary. Why can't everything just be in its place? Why can't the 'good days' be my whole reality? These are some questions I ask at times. I still go through things that aren't pleasing to me and in those moments, I feel like throwing in the towel. There are days I feel depressed because of the process, and I lose focus on the finish line. One of the reasons we wallow in the challenges of the process is because we lose sight of the end result, the goal. The major objective in a soccer game is to score a goal. It really doesn't count how much you dribble your opponent or how good your pass was. Of course, these are good tips to score a goal, but the main focus is on the goal post and that's where everyone is aiming. If we concentrate too much on the obstacles, we will lose sight of the goal. In the same way, if we focus on the obstacles on our journey, we can lose sight of our goal. If your goal is to overcome fear, pass a course in school, start a ministry or even start a business, you have to be focused on whatever you're aiming to achieve. As we continue to live in this world, there will always be distractions. Distractions can be the pain you feel in the process or the doubt, discomfort, fear, etc. But we can decide to press on regardless and say 'though it may be painful, what I'm about to give birth to is joyful', 'though it may be uncomfortable, what's at the finish line will bless lives', 'though it may hurt, what God is bringing out of it is going to break generational curses'. You may just be that one person in your family who has to press on to bring healing. You may just be that one person who has to go through every pain to birth the purpose that will lead others to step into their calling. You may just be that one woman, man, boy or girl, who has to strive and decide that everything that's negative ends with you. The curses, the diseases, the hardships, those chains - they can't move over to our kids! You may just be the one to say 'I'm choosing to go through every process I need to go through for the blessings to come.'

Before embracing a process, there must be recognition. Many times, we spend years in situations because first, we haven't recognized that we have a problem. Also, we haven't accepted that it is a problem that can be solved by God. Identifying our problems is a step to embracing the process which leads to your solution. I have been through a journey that made me feel like healing wasn't possible. I have been through processes of overcoming my insecurities that didn't seem feasible. Sometimes, I feel the enemy's lies-that I can't be made whole, or I can't scale through. There have been times when I almost settled for what felt safe, because I felt like the process wasn't something I had the capacity to embrace. There were times I felt like 'maybe this is just how I am meant to live throughout life-sick, disconnected from God, dealing with addictions, insecurities and depression'. But I pressed on, and I am still pressing on. It may not be easy but I'm still moving and making progress. Little steps to freedom are still steps to freedom. If we truly desire freedom, godly success, victory, etc. we must be willing to step into the process.

If you ever feel like anything you're dealing with cannot come to an end, I want to tell you that it is a lie that the enemy is using to trap you. Of course, the enemy doesn't have your best interest at heart. All he wants to do is to kill, steal and destroy. We must be so zealous in attaining the goal that we are willing to go through any process God has for us. I understand that when the process gets tough, we may feel like returning to who/where we used to be because we were comfortable there, even if it wasn't the best. Just like the Israelites, they rejoiced when they were loose from the captivity of the Egyptians but later got into a pensive mood when it was time for them to embrace the process of getting into the promised land. There is always a promise but there is also always a process to the promise land. We cannot bypass the process if we truly want to attain the promise.

Oxford Dictionary defines process as a 'series of actions or steps taken in order to achieve a particular end'. The process to your goal is a journey, which means that there must be movement to attain the goal. Sometimes we remain stagnant in our journey because we are not willing to take actions that will take us to the next level. I view 'process' as climbing a staircase which requires you to move, step by step, to the top. In life's journey, as we climb, we get a greater perspective for what's ahead. Each step teaches us a lesson to apply once we reach our destination. The blessings have already been prepared by God and they are waiting for you to come get them. But it is what you learn in the process that will help you avoid squandering the blessing.

Every process is for our own good, to make us equipped and ready to make good use of the blessings. God never intend to delay us in any way. It is all in His timing. It's true that sometimes we can prolong our waiting season or our process when we become disobedient to God's instructions. That is why we need to partner with God and listen to every instruction He

118

gives for each step. We must understand that God is speaking every moment, and we are expected to listen. I listened to a sermon and the pastor said, "If all you are moving with is what God told you five years ago, you probably have missed some of His recent instructions." I totally agree. God is a dynamic God. This means that He does His things as He chooses to do them. Think about Abraham. If Abraham wasn't listening to God for every step He made, he would have killed his son Isaac without realizing that God had provided a ram for the sacrifice. Do you know we can sometimes obey God with an angry heart and then miss the next instruction that could be in our favor? Abraham was willing to listen to God in his process of obedience. In the same way, we should be willing to listen to God when we are in the process to getting the blessing.

Truly, deliverance and freedom awaits us if we stay committed to the process. Trusting God in the process can get difficult but we must be committed to the journey of getting our freedom. I could have given up long ago when it came to my freedom from fear, insecurities, etc. If I had given up and chose to settle for the enemy's lies, I probably wouldn't have written this book. If I chose to give up on my dreams and wallow in depression, I probably wouldn't have started my ministry. If I gave up on what God has placed inside of me and decide not to step into my calling, those assigned to me wouldn't have been blessed by what God has given me to bless the world with. If I decided to be lazy and not embrace the process to my breakthrough, I probably would have been lost. Today, I want to remind you that Jesus didn't give up on you, so you don't have to give up on yourself. Jesus went through every process, painful and undeserving, yet He chose you over His comfort. He could have given up on you in the process of bringing you freedom but, He saw a future you couldn't see. He saw a future of you walking everyone around you to freedom. He saw a future of you helping others break generational curses. He saw a future of you being a blessing to your generation. He saw a future of the one He loves dearly, and He decided to embrace any process, as hard as it was, just to bring you the freedom that you needed. If Jesus didn't give up on your future, you can't give up on your future. If Jesus didn't give up on your calling, you can't give up on your calling. You have to press forward! Embark on that journey to your freedom. Embark on that journey to your breakthrough. No fear, just Faith!

The process is a refining phase where every unnecessary thing is removed in order for it to be its best self. Think about the refining process of gold. The gold is separated from the cyanide solution and smelted to remove some of its impurities. The process God allows you to go through is a refinement process that produces the best of you, that matches the best for you-His blessings.

"He will sit as a refiner and a purifier of silver; He will purify the sons of Levi, And purge them as gold and silver, That they may offer to the Lord An offering in righteousness."
Malachi 3:3 NKJV

The process is God purifying you to be better. Just like a potter, He is molding and reshaping you to be the real person He created you to be. I don't know about you, but whenever I receive a blessing after the process, I thank God for the process. It's not just enough to pray for God's blessings, but also, we have to pray for the grace to go through the process that will teach us how to make good use of the blessings.

"And patient endurance will refine our character, and proven character leads us back to hope."
Romans 5:4 TPT

This Bible verse explains how we need to be patient in the process. Sometimes, we are ready to embark on the process, but we aren't willing to be patient if the process prolongs the time we have set in our minds. One truth we need to always remember is the fact that God's timing is not our timing. God wants us to trust Him 100% and not just trust Him to work in our timing. It is in the process that we build character which reflects the fruits of the spirit. Having the gifts of the spirit is good but what sustains it is the fruits of the spirit in us. In this season of waiting, God is refining your character to fit the blessings. When the Israelites went through the wilderness, it was a season that God wanted them to trust Him fully. God wanted them to have faith in Him and know that if He could bring them out of Egypt, then He can take them to the promised land. Out of disobedience, many Israelites were unable to get to the promised land.

If we get so interested in the finished product that we become absent in the process, we may also remove ourselves from the promise. Now, I am in no way trying to degrade how you feel about the process. I have been there before and even right now, there are days it feels like everything is falling apart. Some days it feels like my prayers are not crossing my roof. Oh, and there are days when I don't even feel like praying or worshiping. During moments like this, try to press on and talk to God about how you feel. He truly sees and knows how you feel about the process. Don't allow the enemy to infect your heart posture. Continue to give it all to Jesus and remember that what's ahead is greater than what you're going through. Remember, the blessings require a healed soul for its usefulness. God wants the best for you and His glory will be revealed soon in your life. Keep trusting and believing. Keep pushing and aiming for the best. Focus on the promise and not the obstacles to the promise. Say this prayer if you're in a process that seem hard and unending:

"Dear Lord, thank you for my life and the process you are putting me through. I believe that everything you allow me to go through is for my own good. I submit my heart to you today and I ask for the right heart posture as I go through this journey. I pray for the grace to embrace your preparation in my life for the blessing that is ahead. I pray for an open heart to receive, an open ear to hear from you and an open eye to see the wonderful things you're doing in my life and the things you're about to do. I receive the grace for sustainability as I remain patient in the process. Thank you, Jesus for what you're birthing in me during this season. Thank you for the unimaginable things you're about to do in me and through me. In Jesus name, Amen."

I just want to let you know that there is beauty after the mess. The process may look messy, but the beauty is coming. Keep pushing until you see a victory!

16

CHAPTER SIXTEEN: VICTORY OVER FEAR

"We all need to know that where the enemy has kept us is not where we belong and until we make a decision to return to the place of victory, we will continue to live in the enemy's custody."

The victory over fear is a victory that was won over 2,000 years ago when Jesus said 'It Is Finished.' What this means is that we already have the victory over fear through Jesus and all we need to do is to walk in the victory. Walking in victory means realizing that you have the victory, and you have received freedom over fear or anything holding you captive. Jesus's death and resurrection means so much in our lives and it just tells us how much God was able to give on our behalf in order for us to be set free from every bondage. It shows us the willingness of God to give us the victory that we needed. What happened on our behalf years ago didn't end there. The victory that was won was meant to be passed down to every generation in the lineage of Christ. This is a certainty. But the enemy is still fighting for one thing: our identity. He can't steal the victory, so he tries to get into our mind and keep us preoccupied with the things of this world that we forget who we are in Christ and the victory that was won on our behalf.

"Stand fast therefore in the liberty by which Christ has made us free, and do not be entangled again with a yoke of bondage."
Galatians 5:1 NKJV

The dictionary defines "Stand fast" as to firmly remain in the same position or keep the same opinion. If Jesus brought us out of the bondage of darkness, which includes fear, and brought us into His marvelous light, which is victory, we have to make conscious efforts, with the help of the Holy Spirit, to never return to the place of defeat. If you're living in defeat, there is a call to receive victory. One beautiful thing about God is that He can meet you where you are. If you're in bondage right now, Jesus can meet you there if you want to be met. And guess what? It doesn't stop at the meeting, it transforms into a faith walk that gradually takes you to where you originally belong, which is the place of victory.

124

Many times, we are held captive because we left our creator to try something else. You may have tried everything, and it didn't work out instead, it held you hostage for years. The only way you can gain the victory again is by returning to the giver of the victory-God.

The story of the prodigal son in the Bible shows us how we sometimes act in our daily lives. We sometimes settle for temporary comfort and merry, and we lose ourselves to the enemy when we should be walking in victory. The prodigal son rebelled against his father and went through suffering until he decided to return home. Returning to where you truly belong is gaining victory over the enemy. Where the enemy has kept you-the place of suffering, fear, guilt-is definitely not where God wants you to be. The enemy has held you in bondage that you now feed on the foods of pigs just like the prodigal son when your father has a beautiful palace. The prodigal son lived like a victim until he came to the realization of who his father is and the better place he has for him.

We all need to know that where the enemy has kept us is not where we belong and until we decide to return to the place of victory, we will continue to live in the enemy's custody. Some of us have lived in fear for so long, that it feels normal. We have been tied down for so long by fear that we refuse to try walking in victory. Listen, just like the prodigal son, it takes a step. It takes a step to victory and God will walk you through it. God is not waiting for you to take all of the steps to get to victory, that might be hard to do. All He wants us to do is to decide. Just a step and He will walk you back home.

"When he came to his senses, he said, 'How many of my father's hired servants have food to spare, and here I am starving to death! I will set out and go back to my father and say to him:

Father, I have sinned against heaven and against you. I am no longer worthy to be called your son; make me like one of your hired servants.' So he got up and went to his father. "But while he was still a long way off, his father saw him and was filled with compassion for him; he ran to his son, threw his arms around him and kissed him."
Luke 15:17-20 NIV

The Bible says, "When he came to his senses...". Some of us need to come back to our senses. Maybe we weren't thinking well when we allowed the enemy to move us out of our place of victory. Maybe we were so frustrated that we gave into the thought of the enemy. Maybe we allowed pain to move us out of God's presence. Just maybe we got so overwhelmed by people not liking us that we forgot to rely on God's love. Maybe we were overworked and were burnt out to the extent that we accepted what the enemy came with instead of resting in the shadows of God's wings. Maybe we weren't dressed in our full armor, and the enemy had a chance to come in. Well, one good thing is that we have a God of second chances. We have a God whose love keeps chasing after us. We have a God who has been extensively looking for the "1" sheep, leaving the 99 behind. Maybe you are the "1" sheep that God decided not to give up on. I don't know about you, but sometimes I am the missing sheep. There are days that I am the lost coin, other days I am the daughter who decides to go away with the blessings of God forgetting that there is more. But the truth is that no matter how lost we are, we can be found. We do not have a God who gets tired of looking for us until we are found. Heaven does not just rejoice over the one soul that repents but also over the souls that find their identity and become authentic. The host of Heaven rejoices over the soul that moves from the place of fear to the place of faith. Heaven is interested in your victory. God anticipates our victory every day. He is a God who already won the victory and wants us to walk in it. God has empowered you for victory and it's time to walk in it. You were built for this! God didn't bring you this far to be a victim but a Victor. The price has already been paid. There is someone who has died so you can have access. It's time to take your position as a child of God.

"Shall the prey be taken from the mighty, or the lawful captive delivered? But thus saith the LORD, Even the captives of the mighty shall be taken away, and the prey of the terrible shall be delivered: for I will contend with him that contendeth with thee, and I will save thy children."
Isaiah 49:24-25 KJV

When the Bible says this, it means even if we caused ourselves pain steaming from the consequences of our actions or disobedience, God will still deliver us from it. Sometimes, what we go through is as a result of the choices we have made. Our choices always have consequences, but God is saying that by His mercies, we will be delivered from anything holding us captive. God is just so good and all He wants is for us to walk in the dominion He has already given us.

To anyone who has been lost in fear for so long, being held by the enemy, God's victory is available for you. I encourage you to know that gaining the Victory over fear is a process and you need to focus on Jesus. I pray that this book blesses you and equips you with the spiritual strategies you need to gain victory over fear. You got this because God got you.

As we move over to the next section, which is our Devotional journal, take your time to be transparent with God and to yourself.

DEVOTIONAL

Seven Days to Victory Over Fear

DAY 1
GOD SEES AND HEARS YOU

Oftentimes, we are so bombarded by fear that we forget that God is right there with us through every step of the way. Fear can cripple our minds and leave us in a state of overthinking about who God says He is. Maybe we have prayed and waited for deliverance for so long that it doesn't seem to be coming.

Let me tell you the truth, God sees you and He knows everything going on in your life. He knows that you are dealing with fear and He is ever present to help you.

I want you to take this time to open up to God. In the spaces provided below, write out every kind of fear you are dealing with. Fear of death, disappointment, the society, your tomorrow, your kids' well -being, your health, your family, and everything else. Truthfully write down how you feel.

BE REAL, BE YOU, GIVE IT ALL TO JESUS.

GOD'S WORD OVER YOUR LIFE

"Fear not, for I am with you; Be not dismayed, for I am your God. I will strengthen you, Yes, I will help you, I will uphold you with My righteous right hand.'"
Isaiah 41:10 NKJV

AFFIRMATION

I affirm that God is in me, with me and for me.
I will not fear.

DAY 2
UNHINDERED BY FEAR

It is almost impossible to hear someone say they haven't been fearful in their entire life. What really changes things is our decision to not be limited by our fears. We have to make the decision to move forward regardless of the obstacles. The aim of fear is to stop us from moving forward but if we decide to move forward regardless, then fear becomes defeated.

Today, write down everything fear is limiting you from doing. Think of the things you would have accomplished if you weren't afraid. Be truthful.

GOD'S WORD OVER YOUR LIFE

"Be strong and of good courage, do not fear nor be afraid of them; for the Lord your God, He is the One who goes with you. He will not leave you nor forsake you.""
Deuteronomy 31:6 NKJV

AFFIRMATION

I affirm that I have the courage to move forward and not be hindered by fear.

DAY 3
UNDOUBTED PROMISES

If there is one thing the enemy wants to do to us, it is to continually keep us in a state of doubt where we no longer believe in God's promises probably because it is taking longer to come. The enemy knows he cannot stop what God has said concerning our lives, so he goes ahead to put doubt in our hearts. God's Word already stated that if we believe, then we will receive. What happens when we don't believe?

Today, I want you to take your time to write down every promise of God in your life. If you can't think of any, go to His Word and find out His promises to His children. When writing these promises, personalize it. Put your name on it and proclaim that everything God has said concerning you will come to pass.

GOD'S WORD OVER YOUR LIFE

"But when you ask, you must believe and not doubt, because the one who doubts is like a wave of the sea, blown and tossed by the wind."
James 1:6 NIV

AFFIRMATION

I affirm that my trust is in God. I refuse to doubt but believe all His promises over my life.

DAY 4
SPEAK IT OUT LOUD

There is something about using your voice to speak your victory into reality. One thing fear does is that it silences our voice to the point that we feel comfortable in it. One of the ways I overcame fear was speaking out and literally speaking back to fear. Listen, those situations and obstacles have ears so you need to send them back to where they belong to by telling them that they do not have a place in your life. You have to speak back God's truth to the lies of the enemy. When Jesus was tempted, He had to respond with God's Word.

Take your time today to not just write down but speak to everything you are afraid of. If the devil keeps whispering lies to your ears, respond now to all those lies with the opposite, which is what God says. For instance: If the enemy keeps whispering that you will die, respond now with what God says. "God says I shall live and not die."

GOD'S WORD OVER YOUR LIFE

"Who can speak and have it happen if the Lord has not decreed it? Is it not from the mouth of the Most High that both calamities and good things come?"
Lamentations 3:37-38 NIV

AFFIRMATION

I affirm that everything God has said concerning me will come to pass. I refuse to be silenced by fear but to use my voice for God's glory.

DAY 5
HE THAT IS IN YOU IS GREATER

Growing up, one of the very first affirmations we learnt was "He that is in me is greater than he that is in the world."

This affirmation reshaped us as little children to believe that God is bigger than anything that tries to harm us. The truth is that we live in a world we do not belong to and we can sometimes feel the great wind from the world that makes it look like we are going to be conquered. God wants us to always know that His spirit lives inside of us and can never allow anyone or anything to harm us. Do you know what it means for the creator to live inside of you? Whenever I think about this, I get marveled by the kind of authority and power we have over the enemy.

Today, I want you to take your time to write down "He that is in me is Greater than" everything or situation you may be going through.

This is an example- "He that is in me is Greater than Cancer"

GOD'S WORD OVER YOUR LIFE

"You, dear children, are from God and have overcome them, because the one who is in you is greater than the one who is in the world. We are from God, and whoever knows God listens to us; but whoever is not from God does not listen to us. This is how we recognize the Spirit of truth and the spirit of falsehood."
1 John 4:4, 6 NIV

AFFIRMATION

I affirm that I am a child of God, and the spirit of God lives inside of me. I refuse to fear anything because my God is greater than any situation that comes my way.

DAY 6
HE PAID IT ALL

Jesus' death on the cross of Calvary was not just to save us from our sins but to also bring us out of every bondage of the enemy. When Jesus said "IT IS FINISHED", guess what He meant? Your fears, guilt, insecurities, addictions, depression and many others have been totally paid for.

You don't have to go through all those issues again, because those were the things He paid for. God knew that we could by no means redeem ourselves from the bondage of the enemy that was why He sent His son, Jesus. One beautiful thing is that we were not redeemed with perishable items such as food or drinks and not even with money that could lose its value. We were redeemed by the blood of Jesus which is still speaking for us and will continue to speak for us.

Today, take your time to write down everything that seems to be holding you captive and respond to it by putting down "Jesus Paid Off With His Blood".

This is an example: "Jesus paid off my sicknesses with His Blood"

GOD'S WORDS OVER YOUR LIFE

"When you were dead in your sins and in the uncircumcision of your flesh, God made you alive with Christ. He forgave us all our sins, having canceled the charge of our legal indebtedness, which stood against us and condemned us; he has taken it away, nailing it to the cross."
Colossians 2:13-14 NIV

AFFIRMATION
I affirm that I will no longer struggle with what I have been redeemed from. Jesus paid it all and I am free indeed.

DAY 7
YOU HAVE THE VICTORY

You have the Victory! That's all I've got to tell you. You need to claim what God has already given to you through His Son, Jesus. No longer will you be held captive by the enemy. It's time to walk in Victory. It's time to have a Victor's mindset and not a victim mindset.

Write down everything you are believing to gain Victory over and proclaim that you have the Victory already. This is an example: "I gain Victory over the spirit of fear and depression."

GOD'S WORD OVER YOUR LIFE

"With God we will gain the victory, and he will trample down our enemies."
Psalms 108:13 NIV

AFFIRMATION

I affirm that I have Victory over the enemy. No longer will I have to struggle with things Jesus already gained victory for my sake.

www.ingramcontent.com/pod-product-compliance
Lightning Source LLC
Chambersburg PA
CBHW071751120626
46550CB00002B/745